KNOW YOURSELF, KNOW YOUR CUSTOMER

The SUCCESS INSIGHTS method for superior sales competency

John A. Butler & Frank M. Scheelen

www.oaktreepress.com

OAK TREE PRESS
19 Rutland Street, Cork, Ireland
http://www.oaktreepress.com

A catalogue record of this book is
available from the British Library.

ISBN 1-86076-239-5

Previously published as **So Gewinnen Sie jeden Kunden**
(Frank M. Scheelen) by Redline Wirtschaft bei verlag
moderne industrie & ueberreuter,
Postfach 50 06 32, 80976 München, Germany.

Use of the Sales Competency Model on pages 61 to 68
is by kind permission of the copyright-holders,
Century Management Limited.

Printed in Ireland by ColourBooks.

CONTENTS

INTRODUCTION

Selling is more complex and demanding than ever before! Customers are better informed and more sophisticated. They have more choices than in the past. Nonetheless, they are still as human as they ever were in terms of how you sell to them.

Using the method we are going to present to you in this book, you will be able to influence and sell to prospects and customers of every kind and description in less time and with less stress. We have used this method for years. We teach it to sales professionals, experienced sales trainers and coaches, sales managers and business owners and always receive a positive response. The SUCCESS INSIGHTS method for superior sales competency is an easily-learned and practical technique, which is fantastically successful. Using it:

- You will become a human relations expert. You will learn how to have a higher order connection to every customer.
- You will be able to evaluate how customers perceive you and adjust your selling style to the special behavioural needs of each customer – with conviction and sincerity.
- More customers will buy from you because you have appropriately influenced them – and your sales figures will reflect this.

Successful sales companies know that the source of their competitive edge lies in constantly improving their products, sales processes and the behavioural attitudes of their salespeople. How competent a company's salespeople are in developing and retaining customer relationships is a decisive factor for the success of any market enterprise. Despite e-Business and Internet technologies, we believe it will be this human behavioural competency that will make all the difference in creating sales advantage in the future. The more products, prices, new developments and advertisements become the same, the more important the role of sales competency in customer relationships. If you recognise how this intangible factor can be a source of gaining sales advantage, you are already on the winning trail.

Today, the customer expects you – and your competitors – to know your product and your market inside out. What will make you stand out from your rivals is your personality. We are not talking about charisma here – that is something some people have and others don't. Our long-standing experience as sales and management consultants has taught us that the extra advantage gained from "the personality factor" has a lot to do with self-knowledge. A person who is aware of the impression they transmit to others will radiate more confidence, calm and conviction. This investment in your own personality development and your corresponding competency improvement in customer relationships will pay a dividend: Sales meetings with customers will run much more easily and you can invest the time and energy saved into acquiring new customers and managing your current customers with more professionalism. And you will automatically increase your sales results.

Become a customer relationship professional everyone likes to do business with!

SELLING TODAY

What is important in the world of selling today? The requirements for conducting successful sales meetings with prospects and customers have changed. Salespeople are faced with a new situation:

- *Customers are better informed*. The salesperson's knowledge is no longer superior to that of the customer. Today, customers have a wide variety of possibilities to collect information before they meet you: via the specialist press, the Internet and experts within their own companies. They will usually have gathered a lot of information before entering into sales discussions.

- *"Trained" buyers.* Nowadays, customers train their buying personnel just as well as their salespeople. Outdated selling techniques will appear formal and unconvincing. Very few will be influenced by them.
- *Distrust of advertising.* Customers want to be seen as individuals and not as part of a mass audience. By now, everyone has developed a certain degree of resistance to advertising and clever sales messages. No one wants to be manipulated. The customer of today wants to be treated as a partner.
- *Invisible decision-makers.* You may never see the key figure(s) who make buying decisions. Or the person you negotiate with may be only one of several decision-makers. This is a realistic scenario in a world where company structures are becoming more and more complex and less and less transparent. And yet you still have to find a way to "reach" these invisible decision-makers with your offer.

Selling is becoming more and more complex. Your customer expects something special from you; otherwise they are going to buy elsewhere. Be one of the best, one of those who realises what matters! *The best possible road to success for you as a sales professional in the future lies in "bonding" customers to you in stable long-term business partnerships.*

Your personality may be the only thing that sets you apart from the rest. Of course the quality of your products and services must be high but, there, your competitors are on your heels. However, if the customer swears by you as "our" business partner, you have beaten the competition. If your customer accepts **you**, you have an added edge for closing the deal ahead of your competitor. Then they will trust you if you recommend a particular solution to them. Your credibility rating will increase your sales figures.

You are probably thinking that all this is easier said than done. After all, each customer is different. Customers' ideas of what constitutes good treatment and a pleasant atmosphere will often vary considerably.

One customer finds it pleasant to chat about their last holiday before getting down to business. Another is not interested in any chat at all; they simply want to be informed as briefly and as precisely as possible about your products or services.

In most cases, if you do not know in advance what expectation your customer has and what sort of atmosphere they prefer, you run a great risk of striking the wrong note and losing them within the first two minutes. But saying "Yes" to everything in order to avoid conflict is not the right method either.

It does not matter to the average customer what type of personality you are or what your preferred selling style is. If you want to close the deal, it is up to you to adapt to their style.

So what can you do? How can you become a top sales professional without constantly changing your colour like a chameleon?

THE SUCCESS INSIGHTS SALES SYSTEM

The SUCCESS INSIGHTS sales system gives "insights" into one aspect of your personality and competency make-up and offers you the chance to optimise your abilities as a customer relationship professional.

The sales competency model outlined below (**Figure 1**) has three parts and shows where this aspect of your personality fits into the total personality picture.

The first dimension is temperament or natural behaviour – the focus of this book. It's about HOW you will sell!

The second personality dimension is about nurture or WHY you are motivated to do the things you do. These are often the hidden motivators and emotional intelligencies that drive successful performance. Many motivational sales books have focused on this aspect of selling. We believe that the attitudinal aspect of selling is well catered for elsewhere.

The third dimension of the sales competency model is made up of the skills you have learned, your education, IQ, environmental influence and your experiences. This is WHAT you have learned and know – your learned practices.

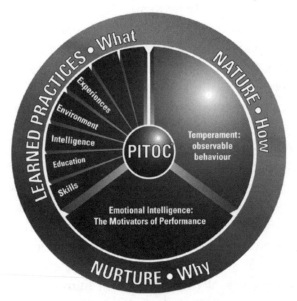

The Sales Competency Model™ provides a total framework to define, measure and develop the competencies of superior sales performance and allows critical sales competencies to be identified, learned and achieved.

Figure 1: Sales Competency Model

Sales competencies are the combination of natural behaviours, attitudes, values, emotional intelligences and learned practices applied by effective sales professionals to deliver superior results. This book is focused on the powerful influence that your temperament – your natural inborn observable behaviour – has on being a competent sales professional.

The SUCCESS INSIGHTS system and the exercises will pinpoint your natural selling style. You will also learn sales methods that you can apply to be successful in your profession. It doesn't have to be the same method all the time! In addition, within a short time you will be able to recognise the behavioural type of your prospects and customers. Thus, you will know their perception of you, what their preferences are, and you can adapt your own style to suit theirs. The SUCCESS INSIGHTS system will enable you to speak the language of your customers – to "connect" with them. You remain who you are, but you can adapt to their style and be understood far more clearly by them.

We predict that you will have more than one "aha" experience while reading this book and putting its content into practice. You will understand why you experience problems with some customers: your difficult customer's "colour" will usually be diametrically opposed to your own. You will learn how to adapt your approach so that you will be able to conduct successful meetings even with these problem customers.

The SUCCESS INSIGHTS sales system is based on the premise that people can be divided into certain temperament styles. Certain people behave in a similar way, and in turn their behaviour clearly distinguishes them from other groups. Without making superficial generalisations, human behaviour can be arranged into clearly identifiable styles. The purpose of this classification is to give a clearer picture of the spectrum of human behaviour. The more you know about the disposition, motives, fears, communication style and the misgivings of your customer, the better you can serve them and meet (or exceed) their needs.

The SUCCESS INSIGHTS sales competency system introduces you to four categories or styles into which human behaviour falls. People in each of these four groups behave, communicate and work very differently. This method is based on the research and study of C.G. Jung, William Marston, Jolande Jacobi and the Myers/Briggs type indicator and uses their insights to develop a model – the SUCCESS INSIGHTS wheel – that can be applied in selling and management situations as well as in putting together the optimum work-team.

To make the four basic styles easier to work with, the SUCCESS INSIGHTS system assigns a colour to each. The basic characteristics of each colour style are:

- Red: The doer
- Yellow: The expressive
- Green: The relationship type
- Blue: The analyser.

To understand the SUCCESS INSIGHTS method, it is at first sufficient to distinguish just four styles. But, in real life, the four basic styles rarely occur in a pure form. Most people are a mixture of at least two styles. So, later, we will consider other blended styles.

Each colour group is particularly suited to one or two of the following eight basic roles (types) in professional life:

- Conductor
- Persuader
- Promoter
- Relator
- Supporter
- Co-ordinator
- Analyser
- Implementor.

HOW CAN THE SUCCESS INSIGHTS SYSTEM HELP YOU?

With the help of this system, you will find out what colour style you are.

- You will learn to recognise your natural strengths and weaknesses. You will be able to apply your knowledge of how others see you and how to avoid misunderstandings. This will boost your own self-confidence and your overall credibility with your customers.

- You will more easily assess the colour style of the customer you are selling to. You will know their preferences, dislikes, how they react under stress and what implicit and explicit language they understand.
- The strategies described will help you to prepare yourself for sales interviews and presentations. You will be calm and professional and your success will be reflected in your increased sales figures.

Moreover, the SUCCESS INSIGHTS system is a valuable tool for finding out:

- Whether the requirements of your job are ideally suited to your personal abilities.
- Whether you can be natural in your job or whether the job description forces you to be someone you are not. In the long-term, this will lead to person-job fit problems that you can recognise and solve well ahead of time.
- Which role you are best suited to in selling and which position in a sales team allows you to make your best contribution.

WHO IS THIS BOOK FOR?

First and foremost, this book is for salespeople – men and women – sales managers, trainers and consultants.

However, the typical behaviour patterns of the four colour styles are, of course, not specific to just the sales profession. Anyone interested in learning more about their personality development and other people will find valuable hints and ideas to significantly improve their communication skills. After all, everyone is in selling! Or influencing! Or communicating! Or persuading!

Remember:

- If you know your "natural" abilities, you can make better use of them. You are far more likely to reach your full potential in the business of selling by working in harmony with your "nature". This is the underlying premise on which we have written this book. We have seen an enormous amount of evidence of the power of the system in more than 20 countries around the world. In different companies, industries, countries and cultures, the "secrets" of this system apply in the same way.

- Faith in your own natural strengths in a career that you love is the basis for success. However, learn to embrace – and study carefully – the opposite side of your natural style also, because hidden energies lie here. In fact, you should develop a new awareness of the aspects of another person that irritate you because these "irritations" could be your final frontier in becoming a fully-rounded personality and sales professional.

- If you can foresee points of tension or conflicts, you can avoid them. The primary reason more of your customers/prospects do not buy from you and put you in the top 10% of your industry is very simple – they do not believe you, or your story, enough to put their 100% trust in your proposition. There has been a personal mis-connection between you – the communications flow is not what it could/should be. The SUCCESS INSIGHTS system is like a filter that maximises the "flow" between the sales professional and their customer.

For centuries, the golden rule of communication has been:

> "Treat others as you would like them to treat you."

Adapted to the world of selling, this means:

> "Sell to others the way you would like to buy."

However, this rule is outdated in this day and age. The SUCCESS INSIGHTS rule of selling is:

> "Sell to others the way *they* would like to buy."

We have written this book to express our experiences of the system in our own countries. People, like countries, are different, yet so very similar. We have spent many days in various parts of the world talking about these ideas and have thoroughly enjoyed the challenge of bringing this book to life. We hope that you will be challenged for the better by reading it!

Be the best you, you possibly can be!

John A. Butler
Frank M. Scheelen

PART 1

WHAT IS YOUR OPTIMUM SELLING STYLE?

1:

RECOGNISE WHERE YOUR STRENGTHS LIE

Peter Greenwood, a senior sales consultant in a software company, has taken over responsibility for a new and important customer. Together with his colleague, Catherine Bell, he pays a first visit to this company. The moment he meets John Redmond, the General Manager of this new customer, Peter realises to his shock and horror that he does not like this man at all. After a cool welcome, they are seated on uncomfortable chairs in front of a huge desk.

Without wasting time on formalities, John Redmond immediately launches into a lengthy lecture on his ideas and wishes. Then he fires off a rapid series of questions at the two sales consultants: Price? Bonuses? Delivery period? Discounts? Installation? Peter Greenwood is angered by this impertinent and impersonal treatment. At the same time, he feels inferior and intimidated.

Catherine Bell, on the other hand, has no problems whatsoever with this customer. She makes notes, answers questions, distributes material and is in full control of the situation. This increases Peter's annoyance. Normally, he is the one who can build up good customer relationships, and Catherine is the more retiring one. And, to add insult to injury, he felt he was most industry-experienced to deal with this customer in the first place. Now he almost wishes he hadn't taken over this key account.

After about an hour, they leave the company. John Redmond saw Peter Greenwood out of his office rather coolly, almost as if he were Catherine's assistant. (It seems quite apparent to Peter that John Redmond did not like him.) As usual, Peter does not say anything, but bottles up his anger instead. They have hardly got into the car when Catherine starts to sing the customer's praises.

"At last, a customer who knows what he wants", she says. "One who speaks his mind. You know exactly where you are with his sort."

Peter cannot understand how she formed this kind of impression. In his eyes, John Redmond is one of those arrogant, rude, man-of-action types who shows no consideration for anything or anyone else.

Have you ever been in a situation like this? You get on really well with a particular customer and your colleague cannot get on with them at all? Why is it that the chemistry is right between certain people and wrong between others? Often, you know after the first three minutes whether someone is "on your wavelength" or not.

You could change that in the future! You could ensure in the first three minutes that the person you are talking to understands and accepts you. And it does not take a miracle. You simply have to look at things through a different pair of (coloured) glasses.

Let us go back to our example. Looking at it through the SUCCESS INSIGHTS glasses, John Redmond is the Red style, Catherine Bell is a Blue-Red and Peter Greenwood the Green style. John is dominating and wants to see results, Catherine is also very practical and seeks clear structures, whereas Peter is the relationship type. He prefers to establish a personal relationship with his customer before he goes on to business. Many customers really like his way of handling things – but not John Redmond. Personal "chatter" gets on his nerves, he always feels he has very little time and he doesn't want to waste what little time he has. People like Peter Greenwood leave him cold.

We all tend to connect better with people who are similar to ourselves. John Redmond and Catherine Bell are similar in most ways, and so were able to find common ground in the meeting. Peter and John, on the other hand, are real opposites. Peter could barely see the positive sides of a customer like John Redmond, let alone turn them to his advantage, because he was too busy looking through his "relationships" glasses.

So a critical sales success factor for Peter lies in his own hands – not to look at his customer through his own glasses but to put **his customer's** glasses on.

If you apply this principle rigorously, you will broaden your horizons (and enlarge your clientele) significantly. If you can interact with your customers as they are, you can change the way you deal with them. If you can see a John Redmond (or a Peter Greenwood) differently and can understand why they act the way they do, you have a much better chance of developing a compatible business relationship with them.

BROADEN YOUR HORIZONS

Study the drawing below. What do you see?

Look again. Can you see that there are two ways of looking at it?

You could see it as the striking profile of a Native American. Or you could see the rounded back of a plump figure in a coat throwing a dark shadow on the wall.

Supposing two different people look at this picture, and each sees only one of the images and does not realise that two pictures are visible! They would argue forever about what the picture shows and only stop when someone told them that they were both right. It is perfectly possible for two people to look at the same picture and each to see something completely different. Something similar happened in the sales talks described above. Catherine Bell saw one side of John Redmond, Peter Greenwood the other. And they were both right, although Catherine Bell found it easier to "appreciate" John Redmond's style.

It depends on our own personal perception of things which side of a picture or a person we see first. Our personality structure, the influence of our past and our conditioning will determine which of the two images we will perceive first.

We see the world not as it really is, but as we ourselves are.

If we can detach ourselves from our accustomed way of perceiving things, we will suddenly be able to see the same object with different eyes. Like the picture: If you see the profile first, it will be difficult for you to make out the contours of the figure in a coat. And as soon as you have seen the contours of the figure in the coat, you can no longer see the profile. To transfer this to our sales talks: If Peter Greenwood had been able to get away from his customary way of looking at things and recognise that John Redmond had absolutely nothing against him personally, but simply wanted to conduct a brief and effective meeting in which he was the one in control, he could have adapted to that style and gone on with the discussion without feeling upset. And he would have won the head and heart of a new customer.

And that is precisely what you will achieve once you are familiar with the SUCCESS INSIGHTS system. You will be able to win over prospects and customers you have preferred to give a wide berth up to now because you simply could not get on with them. You simply didn't like them or sensed they didn't like you.

The famous "aha" experience when your way of looking at things "switches" is the crucial moment. It is the moment when we transcend our customary frame of reference and find a different perspective on the world. Of course, things are not always as easy as looking at the picture was. It will take Peter Greenwood a bit longer to be able to see John Redmond from a different perspective. When it means changing principles, long-standing convictions or deep-seated experiences, we set up a mental block against accepting a new perspective. In these circumstances it takes a good "insight" of self-knowledge and a knowledge of why we see things the way we do before we can free ourselves from our accustomed way of looking at things. We have to learn to take off the colour glasses through which we are used to seeing the world and put on a different pair, or sometimes even many different pairs.

Why should you do this? Why should you move away from your customary perspective? If you really know yourself (know how you see yourself) and how you "know" other people and how others see you, you will see why you have difficulties dealing with some people. And then you can consider more specifically what you would like to change.

A SMALL CHANGE WITH FAR-REACHING EFFECTS

Let's put this in its proper perspective! We are not talking about questioning the way you have acted up to now and turning your personality inside out. It is simply a question of broadening your scope of action, and of removing some of the barriers you have come up against every time your customary perspective reached its limits.

Often, a small change is enough to make a big difference. Think of horse-racing. The winning horse often only wins by a nose. Or the 100-meter sprint. Why do the runners sprint down the home straight with the upper part of their bodies stretched forward? Because they are trying to gain that tiny lead that makes the big difference. Afterwards, no one asks how many centimetres or how many hundredths of a second separated first from second place. Afterwards, all that people remember is who became world champion or who won the Olympic medal.

So perhaps you will have to change your behaviour only very slightly to become one of the best. Follow the "winning edge principle": Even the smallest lead will win the race. Perhaps your competitor's product is just as reliable, the service they offer just as efficient, their prices the same. But your winning edge could be that you get on with your customers better because they feel that you understand them. That's why they will buy from you.

You may not have to change very much at all. Perhaps it will suffice if you just take advantage of a few of the numerous tips and strategies that will be introduced in this book, for your contact with customers to improve decisively. Your sales figures will probably rise noticeably if you are just able to close deals with those customers whom you have found difficult so far. Creating perceptions about yourself as a sales professional consistent with your customers' primary beliefs and disposition will dramatically increase your credibility and positioning in your customers' minds. A huge trust flows from this kind of relationship and trust is the bedrock of all sales success.

It cannot be stressed often enough how important it is to reach customers on a personal level. That is the only way to arouse their enthusiasm. In his best-seller *Customers Only Buy from Winners*, Hans Christian Altmann quotes studies carried out by Rolf Berth which prove that:

- "Emotional enthusiasm" is decisive for sales success
- Only 33% of deals in industry and only 21% of deals in consumer markets are closed as a result of reasoned and logical argument
- In contrast, 67% of all deals in industry and 79% of all deals in consumer markets are closed because the sales professional has succeeded in fascinating their customers and arousing their enthusiasm.

And so the all-important question is: How can you make your customers enthusiastic?

What awakens **your** enthusiasm? I'm sure you find it very positive when the person you are talking to gets involved in the way you like to conduct meetings. Let us assume you are someone like John Redmond: You want to see results, you do not want to waste time chatting and you want clear and comprehensive information. You would prefer to do business with a salesperson who caters to your needs: who leaves personality issues in the background, suggests good solutions and is not offended if you do not put on a friendly face. In short: a salesperson who recognises your personality style and adapts their methods accordingly.

You can press the "enthusiasm" button of your customers if you know what makes them enthusiastic, and how they would like to be treated. And to do this, you have to know their personality style. Then you will know how they see you and what you will have to change in order to be able to connect better with this particular customer style.

So, learn to understand the four colour styles and the mixtures of these types better. The SUCCESS INSIGHTS colour system (**Figure 2**) with its four quadrants (and the eight main types) offers a visual and easily-remembered aid in clearly distinguishing four different behaviour patterns and needs structures.

However, there are two points you should always bear in mind when you are working with this model or analysing yourself and others:

- The model only analyses observed behaviour or temperament. Education, experience, moral concepts, skills, attitudes and emotional intelligence are another subject altogether. So do not draw hasty conclusions about someone's whole personality from the SUCCESS INSIGHTS system. And beware of clouding the issue by mixing your own value judgements with your observations.

- It follows that the SUCCESS INSIGHTS classification implies no value judgement. Red is not better than Green and Blue is not worse than Yellow. The classification into four groups is merely an instrument to improve personal, interpersonal, team, organisation and customer communication.

CHARACTERISTICS OF EACH COLOUR STYLE

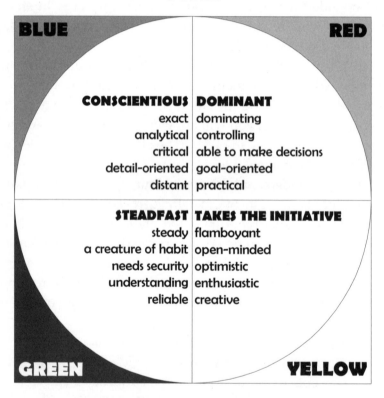

Figure 2: The Four Behavioural Styles

This wheel divided into the four quadrants gives you a first impression of the four behavioural styles.

The Red style

"Reds" like to take action and make decisions. They react quickly and concentrate on taking care of the most important and urgent tasks. They tell other people what they think, sometimes in an almost authoritarian manner. A Red salesperson always knows, or thinks they know, in advance what their customer needs. They have a natural strength and like to be in control of all situations. They tend to be very critical and to prefer challenges where they can test and make use of their strengths. Haggling over the price with a customer is not a problem for this style. The most difficult customers for Red types are those who dither and delay, who cannot make up their minds and then draw back. They get offended when the Red tries to make the decision for them.

The slogan of the Red sales professional could be:

"Let's do it now, and let's do it the way **I** want."

The Yellow style

"Yellows" are sunny and optimistic. They love meeting new people. They are creative and want to make their dreams reality. The Yellow salesperson likes to chat about this and that, before they get down to business. They can sometimes have a bit of a grasshopper mind and for this reason they can sometimes seem superficial to others. The solutions they propose to their customers are often ingenious, though they can also be unrealistic. The most difficult customers for the Yellow salesperson are those who fuss about details, who don't let themselves get carried away with the excitement of a new idea but try to pin it down with clinical questions.

The slogan of the Yellow sales professional could be:

"Let's have fun and kick around a few ideas together."

The Green style

"Greens" have a strong need for consistency and security. They concentrate a lot of attention at the caring level, on relationships between people. A Green salesperson is extremely good at dealing with customers, by putting themselves in their customers' shoes and, by asking the right questions, finding out what the customer really wants. In doing so, they can radiate a lot of warmth. They are very good at following up and are very reliable. The only customers they have difficulty with are those who are impatient, and those they cannot establish personal contact with.

The slogan of the Green sales professional could be:

"Let's treat each other well and act with conviction."

The Blue style

"Blues" always analyse every aspect of a question thoroughly before they form a judgement. They act on the basis of a polished and well-thought-out strategy. A Blue salesperson is always an expert in their field. They know every detail of their product and the answer to every question. However, they may appear somewhat distant to others, because they prefer not to establish a personal relationship with customers. The problem customers for the Blue sales professional are the chatterers who never seem to come to the point but always ask something personal, something that has nothing to do with the business in hand.

The slogan of the Blue sales professional could be:

"Let me think about it carefully and then act according to a precise plan."

In order to be effective in sales, you have to be aware of how you appear to other people. And to do this, you first have to know yourself – your natural colour style. So, after a short digression on the development of the SUCCESS INSIGHTS system in Chapter 2, the following chapters will show you how to define what style of salesperson you are. You will receive an abundance of further information on the four styles and you will have the opportunity to analyse yourself several times. Here is your first chance to undertake a self-analysis.

EXERCISE:
HOW DO YOU SEE YOURSELF?

Take another look at the quadrants in **Figure 2** and think about the descriptions of the four colour styles.
Spontaneously, which style would you say you are?
  The description of the _____ style fits me best.
Were you thinking of the way you act as a salesperson or at home? Or do you behave differently at home?
  In private life I am more the _____ style.
  As a salesperson, I am more the _____ style.
If you could choose just one word from "your" quadrant (or your two quadrants), which would it be?

Write down examples from your private (professional) life where these characteristics were an advantage and a disadvantage for you.

The precondition for self-knowledge is self-observation. So, in future, when conducting a sales meeting, observe yourself and the effect you have on your customer. Of course, this should not demand all your attention and deflect you from the business in hand, but after a while you will begin to develop a sound instinct for your own behaviour. Self-awareness in this manner is a secondary process to the primary sales process but it's what separates the amateurs from the professionals in the career of selling. Limited or narrow awareness often leads to a transaction-type sale or an over-concentration on the product/service features. Total awareness leads to more active listening, a solutions focus, and the possibility for a true partnership-type relationship.

A checklist is often a useful tool. You can ask yourself these questions after every sales conversation. Keep the answers and compare the results when you have taken a closer look at several of your sales interviews. You will doubtless find some behavioural patterns that are quite typical for you as well as others which depend very much on the individual situation.

CHECKLIST FOR SELF-OBSERVATION

How was your manner in your first contact with the customer?
Did you feel confident? If not, why not?
What did this customer expect of you?
Did you indulge in small talk with your customer or did you get down to business straight away? If you did not make small talk, why not?
Were you satisfied with your presentation? Why (not)?
How were your tone of voice and body language during the presentation?
How did you react to the customer's questions?
Were you pushed for time? Why?
Did the customer's objections put you under pressure?
How did the sales interview finish? With what feelings did you leave?

2:

THE SUCCESS INSIGHTS SYSTEM

If background theory does not particularly interest you, feel free to skip this chapter and carry on with reading the next one. Even without knowing who developed the SUCCESS INSIGHTS system and the psychological framework it is based on, you will have no difficulty establishing which type of salesperson you are and which strategies suit you best. You can always come back to this chapter later. However, if you want to know more about the ideas behind the system and why the four colour quadrants (the styles) are divided to form the eight basic types (the types), then this chapter is for you. Keep in mind that the SUCCESS INSIGHTS system is one aspect of the overall sales competency model.

WHAT HIPPOCRATES TAUGHT US

Have you heard of Hippocrates? He was a Greek physician who lived in the 4th century BC and who is considered as the founder of medical science. He was gifted with keen powers of observation and was in the habit of writing down his findings – he was probably a Blue style – a fact for which those who came later can be thankful, because it meant that they were able to build on his observations and develop them further. He is also the founding father of the SUCCESS INSIGHTS system, as well as all theories of personality that explore typology.

Hippocrates classified his patients into four temperaments, depending on which "humour" or body fluid influenced them most strongly:

- *Choleric*: Choleric people are most influenced by gall: It gives them dominance and authority. Choleric people lay claim to leadership – and if they do not get it, they become angry, and their tempers are easily roused.
- *Sanguine*: Sanguine people "consist of blood". This is how Hippocrates describes all loud, optimistic, happy people with a lot of energy and charisma.
- *Phlegmatic*: Here, it is phlegm that influences the temperament. Its effect is calming; phlegmatic people are peace-loving, well-balanced people who tend to remain passive. They do not like to get involved in conflict and will go along with the wishes of those around them.
- *Melancholic*: Hippocrates believed that it was black gall that determined a person's intellectual depth. Melancholy people are liable to suffer from depression and need organisation and system in their lives. Because this is not always possible, their moods are subject to great fluctuation.

Today, we no longer attribute moods to the influence of body fluids. Nevertheless, Hippocrates' observations on human behaviour still retain their validity. With its distinction of four styles and their basic character traits, SUCCESS INSIGHTS is treading in Hippocrates' footsteps: it is a method that has its roots in his observations.

C.G. JUNG:
THE FATHER OF MODERN TYPOLOGY

The Swiss psychoanalyst Dr. Carl Gustav Jung was one of Hippocrates' most talented successors. Striving for a better understanding of human behaviour, he tried to classify personality types and reduce them to a few basic groups. In 1929,

he published his work, *Psychological Types,* in which he names two key aspects under which he examined personality:
- Attitudes
- Functions.

Attitudes ...

Attitudes are a human being's obvious preferences for the "inner" or "outer" world. The "outer" world referred to is understood as the objective world of material things, the "inner" world as a person's feelings, values and ideas. Someone who is "introverted" is more preoccupied with their inner life, with his or her feelings, values and ideas. However, this does not mean that someone who is introverted is necessarily shy of people or egoistic. The attention of an "extrovert" is directed more towards the external world. And so the terms "introvert" and "extrovert" describe whether a person directs their energies inwards or outwards.

... in combination with Functions

Jung also distinguished four basic psychological functions of thinking, feeling, sensation and intuition. These functions must always be seen in combination with the attitudes: Each of the four function types can also be introverted or extroverted. Thus, Jung saw eight basic personality types:

1. Introverted sensation	5. Extroverted sensation
2. Introverted intuition	6. Extroverted intuition
3. Introverted thinking	7. Extroverted thinking
4. Introverted feeling	8. Extroverted feeling

Carl Jung believed that the core of every personality had its "engine-room" in these types. Many other typology models were based on his eight personality types. In few cases can this be as clearly seen as in the case of the SUCCESS INSIGHTS system, which refers to the work of W.M. Marston and C.G. Jung.

MARSTON'S FOUR LETTERS

One of Jung's lesser-known contemporaries was the American psychologist, Dr. William M. Marston. In 1929, he published his book *Emotions of Normal People*, in which he developed the four quadrant model, which today is also known as the DISC model. Marston observed human behaviour and classified four different behavioural patterns: Dominant – Influencing – Steadfast – Conscientious (hence the acronym, DISC). It is important to note that these are behavioural patterns and thus not classified *per definitionem*. These behavioural styles exist, irrespective of the name, in the "real" world.

To allow easier identification, four different colours were later assigned to the four behavioural patterns:

- Red – Dominant
- Yellow – Influencing
- Green – Steadfast
- Blue – Conscientious.

Now you are familiar with another of the components that make up the SUCCESS INSIGHTS system.

JOLANDE JACOBI:
THE INVENTION OF THE WHEEL

Dr. Jolande Jacobi, a disciple of Jung, brought together Jung's typology model and Marston's behavioural styles in 1942 and developed her own model: the Jung-Jacobi wheel. This was an ingenious invention, as it gave Jung's basic personality types a visual form. In addition, the model shows how close together individual behavioural patterns lie and that they can, in fact, overlap.

In this book, we refer to the four colours as the four "styles" (the Marston school) and the eight occupational/professional positions as "types" (the Jung-Jacobi school).

MYERS AND BRIGGS:
THE INVENTION OF SUBTYPES

The two American psychologists, Katherine Briggs and Isabel Myers, are two further spiritual mothers of the SUCCESS INSIGHTS system. They, too, took up the eight Jungian personality types and subdivided each into two subtypes.

Each of the eight types comprises characteristics of its opposite personality type. The individual personality is determined by the mixture of the two – in other words, by how strong the individual characteristics are. You may be familiar with the MBTI Test (Myers/Briggs Type Indicator), based on these types, used today by many companies to test applicants for particular jobs.

THE SUCCESS INSIGHTS SYSTEM

Now you know the family history of the SUCCESS INSIGHTS system, and it is time you heard about the method itself.

An American named Bill J. Bonnstetter developed the first comprehensive software programme that quickly and reliably detected and classified behavioural tendencies using the methods of Jung, Marston and Jacobi. Bonnstetter and his team extended the existing systems to include up to 60 possible temperament positions and provided constant testing and research to support their findings. Their specially developed computer software carries out individual analysis of personality potential (24 pages, including precise colour analysis). Today, with these psychometrics, you can have your behaviour analysed objectively. You can also have a programme of further training tailored to suit your team or company's requirements.

What does the SUCCESS INSIGHTS system reveal?

The system analyses the behaviour of four colour styles and eight professional temperament types. It proceeds from the premise that the uniqueness of an individual arises from a multitude of identifiable and quantifiable character traits. It is this combination of preferences, convictions, fears and particular ways of behaving, or indeed the presence or absence of them, which essentially define the individual temperament. Thus the SUCCESS INSIGHTS system provides a practical framework within which you can classify your own behaviour and that of others. It leads to a better understanding of self and others, and in the end it enables us to communicate better with a wide group of "different" people.

Perhaps you have always mistrusted these "labels", or have been unwilling to accept being classified as belonging to a particular style or type. You may feel that such a classification can never do justice to the uniqueness of your personality, and you are right in this. Nevertheless, being able to see yourself, at least approximately, in one of these styles can be of advantage because:

- You will get to know yourself in a far more comprehensive way, as well as understanding the origin of your talents and motives.
- You will learn to use your strengths *consciously* and *consciously* to avoid your weaknesses.
- You learn how to observe human behaviour and to recognise general personality styles or professional types in other people. This will enable you to predict how someone else is likely to react in a whole series of situations. And being aware of your own temperament style, you will also know how a particular person is likely to react to you.
- From the outset, you can deal with people in a way that suits their style. In other words, you will learn to speak *their* language and can communicate better with them.

What do the four colour styles tell us?

The SUCCESS INSIGHTS system uses preference as a basic yardstick to distinguish characteristic behavioural patterns. (See also Bill Bonnstetter's book, *The Universal Language*).

Extrovert and Introvert

"Extroverted" people are not necessarily the life and soul of every party. It is true that the external world fascinates them more than soul-searching, but that does not mean that extroverts are always gregarious, even if this is usually the case. Extroverts gravitate more towards material things, and are influenced by external factors. Extroverts enjoy the challenge of new projects. They like to be in the limelight and are more interested in the external framework of a task than in its actual content. Salespeople tend to be more extroverted types.

"Introverted" people are not necessarily shy and reserved. Introverts prefer to fix their attention on their inner world, on their ideas, values and feelings, although this does not mean that they automatically shun the company of other people. However, introverted people find it relatively easy to ignore external diversions and can occupy themselves with a subject matter for a long time, alone and with full concentration. They are far more interested in the content of a task than in its external aspects. In general, buyers are more likely to be introverted than salespeople.

To what extent are you Red, Yellow, Green or Blue?

Each of the four colour styles displays the whole range of human behaviour. Everyone gets angry, everyone can empathise with other people, everyone can be very correct, and everyone is creative and spontaneous at some time. But not everyone does so to the same extent. It is the **extent** to which an individual displays a particular type of behaviour that constitutes the difference between the four colour styles – and it is this that will help you to determine more easily to which colour group someone belongs.

Take a closer look at the emotions which are dominant in those around you and it will not be long before you can distinguish the four styles:

- *Red*: The dominant emotion of Reds is anger. If things do not go just as they imagined, Reds are quick to fly off the handle and let others feel their displeasure. The stronger the Red elements are in a personality, the quicker that person will lose their self-control. This is a relatively easy way to judge how dominant the Red aspects are in someone's personality: Do they get worked up about trifles? If so, then you are in the presence of a "bright Red" personality, and now you know how to deal with them. And the opposite is also the case: someone who never loses their cool will have a low proportion of the Red temperament in their personality make-up.

- *Yellow*: You will recognise the Yellow style by their laugh, because the dominant emotion for this style is joy. The Yellow style has an infectious, joyful attitude to life and can fill others with the same optimism, even if the facts do not seem to support it. Is the person you are talking to on top of the world and full of enthusiasm, even though the situation does not really justify it? Then they have strong Yellow characteristics. And *vice versa*: If someone is by nature a doubter, a sceptic, melancholy, then the Yellow element in their personality is relatively low. So, pay attention to how openly someone shows their feelings: The more they "reveal", above all the more enthusiasm they show, the more dominant Yellow is with them and you now know the best way to deal with them.

- *Green*: Greens seem absolutely unmoved and unemotional. Even when everyone around them is jumping for joy, the most you will get from this person is a friendly and sympathetic smile, but they will never get carried away. And *vice versa*: when those around them are depressed and frustrated, the Green personality stands like a rock in a tempest. Greens are in fact very emotional people, but they show those emotions only to their close friends and within the family. So, if you are talking to someone who seems unusually stoic and composed, more so than the situation indicates, you can be fairly sure that the Green temperament is dominant in this person and you can deal with them accordingly.

- *Blue*: The dominant emotion for this style is fear. Although the Blue obviously does not express this openly, it is obvious from their refusal to take any chances or to risk trying anything new. A Blue-style temperament needs to know in advance all the possible consequences of their actions, otherwise they will assume the worst. You can identify the Blue style by their insistence on taking their time over decisions, on getting as much information as possible beforehand, carefully weighing up advantages and disadvantages and limiting the risk as far as possible before they make up their minds. And it follows that people who throw themselves into new ventures without hesitation and without first considering the possible outcome will have a relatively low Blue temperament in their personality.

It is clear that the dominant emotions of two opposite styles will almost cancel each other out: A Red temperament style with a high Green element or a Yellow style with a high percentage of Blue characteristics – it seems almost impossible. "A quick-tempered poker-face" or "A cautious daredevil" are contradictions in terms. However, nothing is impossible, and so some personalities do unite these contradictory emotions within them, though in fact you will rarely encounter such people.

THE SUCCESS INSIGHTS WHEEL AND THE FOUR COLOUR STYLES

Following the example of the Jung/Jacobi wheel, the SUCCESS INSIGHTS system represents the four behavioural styles as a wheel (**Figure 3**). The lists of characteristics help you to see at a glance which colour style describes your temperament. Most people are combinations. People whose personalities display the elements of only one colour type are rare. More common are personalities displaying elements of neighbouring styles.

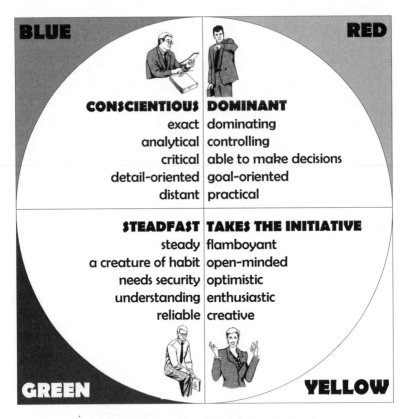

Figure 3: The Four Behavioural Styles

Looking at the wheel, it becomes obvious that there could be overlapping sectors. For example, between the purely Red temperament and the purely Yellow, there is the Red-Yellow mixed temperament.

The eight types you see in the illustration below are the eight main professional types. You have already read a short description of the four colour styles. The eight modern roles that these people like to assume in professional life have been assigned to these colour styles.

Figure 4: The Eight Professional Types

The Conductor

The Conductor is the pure Red type – the doer who likes to set the pace. The Conductor fixes targets and achieves them, too, but often without much consideration for the concerns of others. They have no difficulty in making decisions, and like to make them alone. They also have no problem drawing attention to other people's mistakes and criticising them. As a salesperson, they may seem somewhat arrogant to their customers, despite the fact that they advise them excellently. If they do not agree with the customer's decision, they will tell them so. The Conductor wants to close the deal as quickly as possible. That is why they will often try to hurry the customer or quickly lose interest in them.

The Persuader

The Persuader is a mixture of Red and Yellow. They like to set ambitious targets for themselves and for others to achieve. But they also try to fill others with enthusiasm for these goals. As salespeople, they have a clear idea of what is good for their customer. However, they do not present the customer with this information from a superior position, but try to win the customer over to their own standpoint. This means they often deliver long lectures and may not give the customer the chance to express their own opinion.

The Promoter

A bright Yellow type, a source of inspiration, Promoters love to be where there are lots of people for them to talk to. As salespeople, Promoters present themselves and their product very well. However, they will often forget the time and their customers' needs. Their gregarious nature is their strong point. They know lots of people and can tell plenty of anecdotes and testimonial-type stories. They are very entertaining and thus very popular but, for their customers, the attraction may wear off after a while. They may have difficulty sticking to the point and closing the deal.

The Relator

The Relator is a mixture of the Yellow and the Green. They have a conciliatory nature, always striving for harmony. They are ideal workers in a team. They always see people first and things second. This makes them ideally suited to customer relations, though they are not particularly comfortable in addressing strangers. They take a while to warm to their customers, but will then foster long-lasting business relationships. They ask a lot of questions and are really interested in understanding their customers. This takes a lot of time, and so the Relator will often fail to "nail the customer down" and pull off the deal.

The Supporter

Supporters are the pure Green type, most at home with a small group of friends and colleagues. At work, they like everything to be clearly defined, and do not like being confronted with too many changes. As a salesperson, they prefer to concentrate on products that they support wholeheartedly. They like to be totally familiar with their products and their customer target group. They devote enormous energy to presenting their products, and it is here that their talent for human relationships comes into its own.

The Co-ordinator

Co-ordinators are a mixture of the Green and the Blue type. They are helpful and obliging, but approach their work very methodically and in a very precise manner. As a salesperson, they like to find more comprehensive solutions, but only in areas they know well. They do not feel comfortable meeting new people all the time, but prefer to work with their own group of regular customers who know and appreciate their qualities. They need a lot of time to work out a solution or prepare a presentation and feel pressurised if they have to hurry.

The Analyser

The Analyser is the cool Blue type, who often seems ice-cold. Analysers do not feel happy in a crowd, but prefer to occupy themselves with things, with systems and abstract topics. As salespeople, they like to fiddle around with ideas, and see themselves as the ideal person to find a tailor-made solution for complex customer problems. However, this takes time, so closing a quick deal is not one of their strong points. They have problems making first contact with customers and winning their confidence, but Analysers' customers, usually companies that require complex systems, hold them in high regard.

The Implementor

Implementors have Red and Blue elements in their temperament mix. They like to consider systems and more comprehensive concepts. They have their sights fixed on a clearly defined goal, and know within what time frame they intend to achieve it. Like the Analyser, their strong point is supplying complex solutions for customers. However, they are not afraid to drive a hard bargain on prices and terms. Sometimes, they become disillusioned when they cannot reconcile the high aims they set themselves in striving for perfection.

CONCLUSION

Now that you understand the background to the SUCCESS INSIGHTS system, you will be better able to identify your own style in the next chapter.

3:

WHAT STYLE ARE YOU?

Selling is the oldest profession! Superior sales performers, everywhere in the world, engage in certain universal principles that have stood the test of time. First you sell yourself, then your product, then your company. This order rarely changes. The first thing your customer sees is you, your appearance and the manner in which you approach them – your observable behaviour. Of course, you are both aware that the main "currency" is the product and that you are both there to solve a business need. Nevertheless, whether consciously or subconsciously, your customer will identify you with your product.

There is no obvious connection between the sound of waves breaking on a beach and the quality of hair-care products. But why then do advertising spots present information on the quality of a hair shampoo against the sensual background of sand, sea and the sound of the waves? Because the primary aim is not to present information but to conjure up associations, the idea being that later, when you are standing in front of the shelves in your supermarket, you will remember that happy beach feeling and choose the shampoo that comes with the song of the sea.

Your aim is that your customer, when faced with the choice between your product and the more or less equivalent product of your competitors, should think of you and your pleasant manner – and choose your product.

So how you behave and the impression you give is critically important. But what facet of your personality do you want to display to your customer? Some people behave in the same way in their private and in their professional lives. But many people are completely different when you get to know them outside the office. Suddenly the competitive salesperson becomes the easy-going, wine-drinking connoisseur who can tell amusing anecdotes about his neighbours. Perhaps you find this difference in your behaviour absolutely normal, or perhaps you are simply not aware of the contrast. Therefore, if you want to consciously change the way you behave, you first have to establish your natural behavioural patterns in private life and at work and establish where the differences lie. This chapter gives you the opportunity to do just that: Who are you exactly? Do you know and understand your nature? And are you someone completely different when you are at work?

WHAT IS YOUR NATURAL STYLE?

Your own concept of yourself tells you a lot about who you are, and how you get along in the world. Later, this concept of "self" becomes more differentiated, while remaining largely within the limits you have already defined.

Your concept of self consists of three aspects:

- *Self-image:* The inner mirror in which you see yourself every day. On some days you see yourself more positively, on others more negatively. If you have just pulled off a big sale, you will have a positive image of yourself. If a sale has fallen through, on the other hand, you will be dissatisfied and angry at yourself.
- *Self-ideal:* This is you as you would like to be. Your ideal self is probably that of a top sales professional with outstanding sales figures, who can handle any kind of customer. Or your ideal picture of yourself is someone who is popular and has a lot of friends. Successful people have a very clear picture of their self-ideal. This is important, since it points you in the right

direction for change. You can only achieve goals if you know where you want to be. Your self-ideal will lead you towards your area of excellence and will guide you towards setting and achieving the goals you would be most comfortable achieving.

- *Self-esteem*: What you think of yourself. Your self-esteem is the motor that drives you. It influences almost everything that happens in your life. It also determines how much you can love yourself and how much confidence you place in yourself. Usually, your self-esteem is lower than it should be. As a consequence, you fail to achieve the aims that your self-ideal craves.

Of course, your concept of yourself influences your temperament or natural style – the way you normally behave. How you see yourself, the goals you are pursuing and how highly you estimate your own value will dictate the way you behave. Your natural style is that part of your nature that you most often display at home in your personal space.

The authoritarian salesman, for example, who can relax at home is showing his natural style there. If he was aware of this fact, he could put it to work to his advantage, by making use of his natural charisma in his job. That would make him more flexible and better able to judge how others see him. This is exactly why it is so important for you to define your natural style.

In some cases, the salesperson who is fighting hard to close business deals, and putting pressure on others in order to achieve her aims, is wearing a mask. Her professional style differs enormously from her natural style – maybe because she is afraid that others will take advantage of her if she behaves at work as she does at home. Again, her self-concept influences the way she behaves towards others in her working life.

And so, when you do the exercises in this and the next chapter in order to see what your natural and your professional styles are, always remember to distinguish clearly between the two. Then you will see for yourself whether there is a divergence between your behaviour at work and your behaviour at home or whether you have a uniform style.

Your natural style is an expression of how you see yourself, your behaviour, your strengths and weaknesses.

➢ So, think of situations in your private life here.

Your "mask", or your selling style, is the way you behave in professional life in order to be successful. It is your "public" face at different times.

➢ So, think of some situations in your professional life where you have worn a "mask".

How Do You See Yourself?

Take the time to do these exercises and analyse the results. Gradually, it will become easier for you to identify yourself with a particular colour style and professional type.

EXERCISE:
IN WHICH DIRECTION DOES YOUR BEHAVIOUR TEND?

Imagine that you are planning to buy a new car. You would prefer a bigger car and are keen on a particular model. Your husband/wife, however, has quite different ideas. How do you tackle the issue?

Do the two of you discuss the question together until you have agreed on a solution?
Do you present your partner with a *fait accompli* and rely on him/her realising in time that yours was the right decision?
Do you keep on and on reiterating your standpoint to your partner until you have persuaded them?
Are you prepared to give in because peace and harmony are more important to you than the car?
Or do you have another way to solve the problem? If so, which way?

EXERCISE:
HOW DO YOU APPROACH A NEW CHALLENGE?

Now imagine you are faced with a new professional challenge. Your company is launching a new model or a new version of a product. It is your task to contact your customers and interest them in the new product. Your company expects you to make use of your knowledge of your customers to generate new marketing ideas for the best way to sell the new product. How do you set about it?

You talk to the marketing people and phone a few of your best customers to get a feeling for how they receive the product and what appeals to them about it.
You sit down at your desk and carefully read through all the information on the new product. Then you draw up a plan of action.
You sit down with a few good colleagues and have a brainstorming session. It takes longer than you expected, but at the end of it you have worked out a few good ideas and you personally enjoyed the meeting.
You delegate the work to a colleague, set him a deadline by which he has to present his proposals to you. Then you work on these proposals to turn them into useful ideas.
None of these methods suits you. You have your own way of dealing with such tasks. Which way?

BEHAVIOURAL TENDENCIES

Consider how you handled the situations in the exercises above. Then look at **Figure 5**.

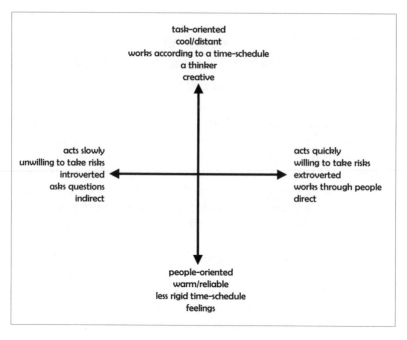

Figure 5: Behavioural Tendencies

1. Which arrow points to the characteristics that best describe your behaviour?
   - In your private life _____
   - In your professional work _____
2. Which arrow points to characteristics with which you are absolutely unable to identify? Why can't you identify with them?
   - In your private life _____
   - In your professional work _____
3. Do your two behavioural patterns differ?
   - Direction of private behavioural pattern _____
   - Direction of professional behavioural pattern_____

Next, look at how you tackle problems or difficult situations – when you have a cool head and are not angry or uncertain.

EXERCISE:
HOW DO YOU MAKE DIFFICULT DECISIONS?

You have been offered a very good job. Professionally and financially, the offer is tempting. Unfortunately, if you accept this job, you will have to move to a new town. You have a wife/ husband and children. Your wife/husband also works and is not thrilled at the prospect of looking for a new job. Your children are in school and are unwilling to leave behind all their friends and their familiar surroundings. How do you set about making the decision?

1. You suggest that the whole family should drive to the new town in order to see whether they like it. In the meantime, you will find the time to discuss the problem and to listen to the family's views. Perhaps your family will be willing to move. Your family is very important to you. If they are not willing to go with you, you will refuse the job.
2. You list all the pros and cons and present it to your family. If the advantages outweigh the disadvantages and are clear to everyone, you think your family will agree to the move. You expect them to be amenable to logical arguments, but you will leave them time to make up their own minds.
3. You are convinced that your family will support your career move. If necessary, you can always spend weekdays in the new town and come home on weekends. You expect your family to make compromises and to adapt.
4. You talk at length with your family and discuss ways to solve the problem. You ask friends what they did in this situation. Through acquaintances, you establish contact with people in the new town and make inquiries so that you can tell each member of your family how he/she can pursue his/her interests and hobbies in the new town. You are sure that you can persuade your family that the move is a good idea.

Which of the four solutions are you most likely to choose? What does this tell you about your style?

EXERCISE:
THE NEW JOB OFFER

Now imagine a situation at work. You are offered a new job as a sales consultant. Financially, it is a step up, and the job has been offered to you in recognition of your achievements. However, in the new sales area, there is keen competition from another company and there are several customers who are known to be tough nuts to crack. It would be your job to boost business with these customers. This job definitely would not be a piece of cake. How do you react?

1. You accept straight away. You like a challenge and you are convinced that you can do it. You are the right person to show these customers who has the best product to offer.
2. You accept because you are sure that someone with the power of conviction can win over these customers. You know that you are eloquent and convincing and that you can persuade these customers to become your customers.
3. You hesitate. You do not like upheavals or great challenges. You are not sure that you could do it. On the other hand, the prospect of building up a relationship of trust with new customers is attractive. You know this is something you are good at and that you have tamed some of the fiercest customers around. You talk to good friends or your family about it, and whether you take the job or not will depend largely on whether they encourage you to accept or refuse.
4. You hesitate. You need time to think about how to tackle such a task and whether you can do it. You gather as much information as you can get about the new sales area in order to get as clear a picture as possible of what to expect. Perhaps you hesitate for so long that they offer the position to someone else in the meantime. However, if you do decide to take the job, your deliberations will stand you in good stead and your chances of success are good. If you are not convinced of this, you will turn the offer down.

Which of these reactions is closest to your own?
Which colour style is this?

Reading the information below on the way the four colour styles solve problems, which colour style fits the way you reacted?

1. *Red type*: The Red reacts quickly, is efficient, decides what is best for themselves, does not waste time worrying about what others think, and seems at first glance to be resolute and hard.

2. *Yellow type*: The Yellow talks to other people, always assumes that everything will be alright, has a multitude of possible solutions for the problem and tries to win others over to their way of thinking.

3. *Green type*: The Green thinks for a long time about what should be done, hangs back, avoids conflict wherever possible, tries to find a compromise and sets great store by the opinions of those they trust.

4. *Blue type*: The Blue assesses the situation, thinks about past solutions for similar problems, plans every step they take and turns a critical eye on their own role and that of others.

Which type comes closest to your way of solving problems?

- In private life: _____
- In professional life: _____

Of course, often there is not enough time to think calmly and logically about solutions when a problem arises. So, consult your gut feeling now, not your head, and consider (in the next exercise) how you react when bad news catches you off-guard.

What have you learned about yourself?

Now draw the conclusions from all these exercises. What is your **natural** style? What colour best fits your **professional** style? Are the colours the same or different?

If your reactions are "mixtures" and even if you have chosen different colours, this is completely normal. Hardly anyone is absolutely fixed in one place. Most of us are mixed styles, and the colour combinations you have chosen should help to pinpoint which mixed style you are.

EXERCISE:
HOW DO YOU REACT TO BAD NEWS?

Let us assume you are having a bad day. It is Friday lunchtime: You have just had an unpleasant confrontation where one of your main customers has given you to understand in no uncertain terms that you will have to lower your prices by 10% or he will buy from your competitors. You have just got back to your desk when the phone rings, and your wife/husband informs you that they have just collided with another car and that your car will be in the garage for repairs for a few days. It seems that that is the end of the weekend trip you were planning. You are both disappointed and livid that this should happen today, of all days. How do you react?

1. The first thing you do is take your temper out on your wife/husband, blaming them for everything. (**Red** style)
2. You criticise your wife's/your husband's driving, then phone the garage to see whether it is possible to get the car repaired sooner after all. You phone an acquaintance who knows the owner of the garage to try to speed things up a bit. (**Yellow** style)
3. Your reaction is more reserved. You withdraw into your shell and expect your partner to do something to save your weekend. (**Green** style)
4. You have your partner explain in detail just how the accident happened, what exactly is wrong with the car and why the garage cannot get it repaired sooner. However, you do not show your anger openly, but more in the undercurrent of your conversation. You are consciously practical and make no reference to your anger. (**Blue** style)

The _____ style fits my reactions most closely.

THE FOUR COLOUR STYLES:
WHO THEY ARE AND HOW THEY WORK

We will now describe the four colour styles in greater detail to make it easier for you to determine your position. We will make a conscious distinction between private and professional style to make it easier for you to decide. In **Chapter 5**, the four styles will be described in clearer terms, as they relate to selling.

The Red style

We all know them: you can tell from a distance that this person is a "doer", that they know what they want and will follow their chosen direction almost unerringly. A decisive personality, a decider who sets clear goals for themselves and who pursues these goals single-mindedly. The only thing that counts is achieving these goals, and the Red will risk quite a lot in the process. In fact, this is the true

The four colour styles

attraction for the Red style. For the pure Red, you are either a winner or a loser, there is no alternative; and it is clear that the Red intends to be one of the winners and will do virtually anything to achieve this objective.

The Red personality style always feels a little bit superior to other people. They have great inborn authority and like to display it. Once the Red has formed an opinion on a matter, their mind is set and it can be very hard to convince them to change. The Red can be extremely critical of others and even ruthless in the pursuit of their goals.

The Red is always interested in the out-of-the-ordinary. They are curious, will usually have a wide range of hobbies and enjoy trying out new things. The Red loves challenge: extreme sports, adventure holidays or risky projects are just the ticket. Others often consider them too fond of taking risks. However, the Red is not one to go in for projects that last too long: Patience is not a Red forte. The Red's diverse interests mean that they like a frequent change of scene.

They like to be active and to act quickly. Irrespective of all logic, in the moment of action, Reds rely very heavily on their gut feeling to tell them what they have to do in order to stay on top. Under pressure, Red styles easily become impatient and tend to "well-founded assumptions" that they recommend with conviction.

In private and in professional life, Reds do not trust other people much and do not confide in many. The Red's personal contacts are usually limited to a chosen few. Above all, Reds are afraid of being used and taken advantage of. As someone whose own interests are very dear to their heart, it would indeed be a bitter moment for a Red to realise that other people had used them for their own purposes and that they personally had not profited in any obvious way.

Workstyle

As far as working life is concerned, only one thing is important for the Red style: that they are the boss. Reds expect others to accept their authority unquestioningly. They find competition very stimulating, as they are convinced that they will win. A Red salesperson considers that they are the best salesperson around, and is sure that everyone else shares this opinion. If the Red salesperson has a boss above them, the boss had better be a Red, too, or at least a personality with strong Red characteristics – otherwise the Red will not respect them and is likely to walk all over them.

Reds like to work alone, even if they are employed by someone else, and they like the challenge of high, medium-term goals, for example the achievement of certain sales figures or winning over difficult customers. The means of achieving these goals, however, must be defined and decided on by the Red themselves. And it is when problems crop up or time presses that Reds really show where their strong points lie. It is no problem for a Red to work out a convincing presentation on one of their customers' problems overnight. Admittedly, however, if there are no problems for them to sharpen their teeth on, Reds tend to create some so that they can solve them.

The Red hates having to do something of which they are not convinced, simply because someone else has ordered them to do it. Correspondingly, other people's opinions do not carry much weight with the Red. They take notice only of the opinions of people they respect. If a Red does not take someone seriously, that person can present the most sensible arguments in the world and they will fall on deaf ears as far as the Red is concerned.

Colleagues and staff are judged according to the same yardstick that Reds apply to themselves – achievement. They respect people who can overcome resistance and who display staying power. They like confrontation and contradict others as a matter of principle. The Red salesperson will even contradict when a customer describes their own company's situation. They like to be the centre of attention and are easily offended if forced to stay on the sidelines. The Red is very susceptible to flattery and not at all surprised that others have such a high opinion of them – they are only confirming what they have known all along.

The Red is are very good at organising and carrying out their tasks, and that is exactly what they expect of others at work. They have no time and no inclination for a quiet chat in passing. When it comes to contact with business partners, they prefer to play tennis with them – and beat them.

As a result of needing to know that they have power – especially decision-making power – in their hands, the Red also needs to check up on others. If a Red discovers that a colleague or one of their employees has made a mistake, they will draw attention to it in no uncertain terms and can be very brusque and sarcastic in the process. This does not mean that the Red is not fair. They are also aware of others' achievements. But, if they make mistakes themselves, however, they have trouble admitting them. Yet, if a Red salesperson suffers defeat, they shake it off quickly. Their self-assurance is indestructible, and they just try harder next time.

One of the things the Red hates most is everyday routine. They will give notice and look for another, more exciting job if they get bogged down in routine and if their present job holds no new challenges. The Red is motivated by difficult tasks, but also by salary increases, promotion or the chance to head an unusual or important project. And they are not averse to titles, a flashy company car, new office furnishings or official recognition of their achievements either.

For a Red at the beginning of their career, it is a great source of motivation if an assistant is appointed to do all the paperwork and the routine tasks. They like compliments and open recognition of their achievements, particularly if expressed immediately. If you ask a Red for advice, you will always get an answer.

At a glance: Tendencies of Red behaviour

Psychological need	To lead others/ management
Outstanding talents	Very self-confident, task-oriented
Aim	Personal goals
Fears	Being used, wasting time
Over-reaction	Impatience

The Yellow style

When you first meet the Yellow, they will greet you with an open, even beaming, smile. They will find the time to inquire about your last holiday trip or to chat about mutual friends. And before you part, they will have a new joke for you.

The Yellow is a "party animal", or at least a very sociable type. The Yellow wants to be liked and will accept others readily –

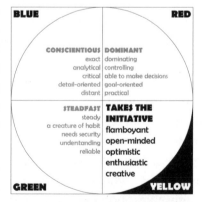

The four colour styles

sometimes unreservedly. They usually have a wide circle of

acquaintances and know everyone in the trade. They are easy to like with their happy, encouraging and vibrant personalities. Their good humour is infectious. They speak eloquently and at length, their presentation is good – and they consider these to be talents, not just habits. They like to be in the limelight, and their eloquence helps to put them there. They try to win others over to their standpoint and will occasionally manipulate them, not out of calculation but because they like talking and are very committed.

The Yellow is often spontaneously filled with enthusiasm for a new idea. Spontaneity plays a very important role in their lives. A Yellow may make plans one day and then throw them completely overboard the next because something new, something better has turned up. This is one reason the Yellow is frequently late for appointments and deadlines. A Yellow has a lot planned and even more in mind, and so it is hardly surprising that their time schedule is sometimes chaotic. They get talking, forget everything else and so are late for their next appointment. But they cannot imagine that the person they have arranged to meet will be angry with them for long for being unpunctual. Their ability to get themselves into trouble is surpassed only by their ability to get themselves out of trouble again!

The Yellow comes alive when they have the opportunity to meet people they find exciting. They are on top of the world when they meet such people, and it does not particularly bother them that most of what they are talking about is fantasy. They carry on spinning ideas, for surely there will be a few useful ones in every hundred. However, because they love entertainment and are therefore easily diverted, they will have trouble seeing their ideas through to the final phase. Often, others profit from the Yellow's creativity by putting their ideas into action.

The Yellow has a tendency to trust other people without reservation, which can sometimes lead to rude awakenings if these people turn out to be less altruistic than they themselves are. Often, however, an inner voice warns them. Remember, Yellows are led predominantly by their feelings. Their strong point is that they seldom do anything that goes against these feelings.

Whatever they do, they need a great deal of recognition from other people. Scepticism throws them off-balance, and they will avoid critics in order not to spoil their good mood. Unless they can convert them to their own more optimistic view, a Yellow will not include people of a pessimistic, negative disposition in their circle of friends.

A Yellow needs that kick. This is probably the colour style with the most bungee and parachute jumpers in it. They are flamboyant daredevils!

Workstyle

The Yellow's workstyle is very clear – they do not have one. They are very creative and can throw themselves with enthusiasm into things that interest them. At the outset, a Yellow salesperson will do everything for a customer they like. They will phone often, and will organise all sorts of things for them. But just as quickly, a good idea will suddenly cause the Yellow salesperson to transfer their attention to another project or another customer. If external forces dampen their zest, they lose all enjoyment and interest in a task.

The Yellow is a born team-worker. They get on well with colleagues and create a pleasant working atmosphere. Their enthusiasm is infectious. They can sweep other people along with them and inspire them to find new ideas. A Yellow boss will sometimes find it difficult to establish his or her authority because Yellows are unwilling to disturb a harmonious working atmosphere.

Concentrating on details is not the Yellow's cup of tea, and they will therefore sometimes skimp on preparation. When preparing for a presentation or important price negotiations, they rely on their strength in making contacts and are convinced they will manage it somehow. They like to improvise, and they often have to because they do not have all the documents they need to hand. They regard putting on a good show in spite of this as a challenge.

Although the Yellow is not keen on going into things at great length and in great depth, they are good analysers of detail. They can turn a spotlight on minor aspects of a project or product if these seem important and entertaining. This often fascinates others.

Yellows can be motivated by providing frequent opportunity for them to interact with others and to work in relaxed, friendly teams. Examples of incentives for Yellows are bonuses, freedom from detail and routine. Acceptance by those around them, frequent conversations with the boss, praise for a job well done, a friendly tone and attentiveness are all very important for Yellows.

At a glance: Tendencies of Yellow behaviour

Psychological need	To work together with other people
Outstanding talents	Optimism, people-oriented, creativity
Aim	Social recognition, to be liked/loved
Fears	Rejection by others
Over-reaction	Chaos

The Green style

On meeting a Green, your first impression is that they are reserved but friendly and obliging. Before they confide in other people, a Green will take a long, hard look at them to establish whether they are worthy of their trust. The Green is not particularly interested in shallow contacts.

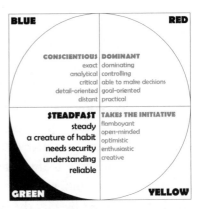

The four colour styles

Once they have decided to trust someone, the Green can be very compassionate and understanding. They are sensitive and empathetic, motivated by a genuine desire to know what the customer requires. They like others to be straightforward, because they are straightforward themselves. Greens become alarmed if others behave ambivalently and give ambiguous signals and will withdraw into themselves if this happens. They are absolutely honest and expect the same degree of honesty from those around them. Their great need for harmony will induce them to seek agreement with others or, in the event of differences in opinion, a compromise. The last thing a Green wants is to hurt anyone by what they say or do, and they have trouble dealing with the situation if others hurt them. They are masters at concealing their anger.

A Green is slow to anger, and seems to radiate an atmosphere of great calm. Their calm nature is their strong point, and it prevents them acting rashly. Their judgement of their fellow-humans is usually balanced and fair. This means they are not easily influenced by other people, but another reason for their caution is their great fear of being cheated. They dislike risks intensely, and bungee-jumping is their worst nightmare. Greens take the safe, tried and tested paths. In terms of adventure, hill-walking or regular golf are more likely to be their hobby. They are usually part of very close families and do not like to be separated from their families for long.

Workstyle

When a Green signs a contract, it is important for them to feel good about it, and so they will consider every aspect thoroughly before signing. A Green approaches all their tasks prudently. Whenever they make decisions, their feelings play an important role.

A Green can only put their talents to full use if they have established a basis of trust with their colleagues and their boss. When they work in a team, they are very loyal and supportive of the other team-members. They like things to be clearly structured and their tasks to be clearly defined so that they know exactly what is required of them. Then they set their sights on their task, draw up a plan of action and work effectively and productively towards achieving their aim. They often develop good and well-established working habits and prefer to work with a fixed group of regular customers. Sometimes, the Green has difficulty setting priorities, tending to think that everything is equally important. They will withdraw if placed under pressure.

The Green has a tendency to take criticism personally. They like to receive praise for their work, but it must be genuine or they will not believe it. If a Green does not like something, they have trouble presenting their case to other people. They will withdraw behind a barricade of passive resistance, often giving a verbal "Yes" but a mental "No". This often makes them seem servile in their attitude to superiors or customers who behave very dominantly, even if this is not really the case.

The Green can be motivated by the provision of predictable tasks, by side-benefits that bring security, by the chance to perform clearly defined tasks and by an harmonious atmosphere. Feedback, particularly in written form, is greatly appreciated by the Green. They like their boss to provide support, clear structures and as much background information as possible about their tasks. A certain percentage of routine does not worry them. On the contrary, they like to know what to expect. Rapid change can paralyse them and trigger fear.

At a glance: Tendencies of Green behaviour

Psychological need	To support others
Outstanding talents	Teamwork, loyalty, result-oriented
Aim	Harmony, clear structure
Fears	Taking risks, being cheated
Over-reaction	Monopolises others

The Blue style

At first, the Blue style is reserved and holds back. They observe other people carefully before forming a judgement. In doing this, they do not mean to be unfriendly, even though they are often misunderstood. Blues feel no compulsion to be constantly making new contacts. They think things over very carefully before entering into dealings with anyone. They like to withdraw into themselves and be alone from time to time.

The Blue needs this time alone in order to be able to think things over at leisure. Once they have thought everything through and worked out the structures involved, they can come up with very well-thought-out, astute judgements and solutions. They have a tendency to analyse many things that other salespeople take as given, and they want to know as much as possible. A Blue's principles mean a lot to them. They act according to the convictions they have formed and are not much influenced by emotions. The Blue is a good judge of character, with a keen nose for errors and misjudgements. Blues set themselves and others very high standards, and

The four colour styles

their great sense of discipline helps them to attain these standards.

In their dealings with other people, respect and mutual regard are very important to them. If a Blue has reached agreements with a customer, they will adhere to these agreements, and will expect their partners in business to do the same. Of course, as a result, they often experience disappointments, and this makes them suspicious and distrustful. It is not easy to win a Blue's trust, but once you have won it, they are not likely to forget it.

Blues are extremely reluctant to talk about their feelings. They have problems finding the right words and they do not confide in their customers. Often, Blues are so inconspicuous and unassuming that others do not appreciate the person behind the facade, do not understand what makes them tick. They most enjoy the company of customers who are very similar to themselves.

Workstyle

The Blue's desk is always tidy. The well-ordered desk mirrors the well-ordered thoughts of the Blue-type personality. At work, they are extremely thorough and exact. They approach things rationally and methodically, first collecting every available piece of information and studying it, and then offering perfect, tailor-made solutions on the basis of the insights thus gained. The Blue prefers to have a precedent on which they can set their sights, and they like their tasks to be clearly defined, so that they know what is expected of them. For a customer who needs an extremely complex solution, the Blue is the right person to work it out. But they need time and cannot be hurried. You should not expect quick answers from a Blue. And you would be wasting your breath if you tried using your authority or power to force a Blue to do something.

Of all four colour styles, Blues have the strongest leaning towards logical thinking and actions. This enables them to recognise possible mistakes in advance and, consequently, to avoid them. Their weak point is that they occasionally get bogged down in the data-gathering phase. They can also react very sensitively to criticism, often interpreting it as a personal slight.

At times, the Blue likes to "pass the buck" on to other people. They will not necessarily try to get involved in any decision-making that has to be done. They find it difficult to make decisions. For them, it has to be the one and only correct solution or none at all, and so they are not keen to take on greater responsibility.

Giving them the time they need to consider the optimum solution can motivate the Blue. They prefer to work alone rather than in a team, although they do need to feel that they are part of a group. They are particularly happy when they are given the chance to develop new skills and expand their knowledge. If a Blue salesperson has to win new customers, they prefer to have the way smoothed, or they smooth it themselves with the help of references. The best recognition of their achievements takes the form of encouragement and praise. They prefer stable, clearly-structured surroundings where they receive clear instructions on what is expected of them and where no pressure is exerted. Sudden changes in their field of activity have a negative effect on their motivation.

At a glance: Tendencies of Blue behaviour

Psychological need	To meet their own high standards
Outstanding talents	Exactness and precision
Aim	Optimum solution
Fears	Criticism of their work
Over-reaction	Overly-critical of self and others

WHICH COLOUR STYLE ARE YOU?

Have these detailed descriptions made it easier for you to identify your colour style? It is time to sum up! Gather together all your conclusions so far, and remember that you do not have to reach a final decision yet! In the course of this book, you will learn a lot more about yourself and you will have repeated opportunities to alter or to adjust your image of yourself and your colour style.

EXERCISE:
YOUR NATURAL STYLE AND YOUR WORKSTYLE

Thinking of the way you act in private surroundings:
Which colour group would you say fits you best now? Why?
Which colour style fits your behaviour at work? Why?
Which other patterns or colour style can you identify from your personal life? Which patterns are they?
Would you say the same of your behaviour at work? What other colour style can you see mirrored here?
Which colour style do you think is the absolute opposite of your private/professional style?
What do you dislike most about these opposite colour styles?
Can you recognise elements of your own personality in them? If so, which ones?
Colour style in private behaviour   _____
Colour style in professional behaviour   _____

YOUR "SHADOW" SIDE

Learning about your opposite colour – your "shadow" side – is vitally important in appreciating the differences in other people and in maximising the opportunity to connect with them. Significantly, your shadow side may represent a disowned side of your own personality and provide an opportunity for personal growth.

DEVELOPING SALES COMPETENCIES WITH THE SUCCESS INSIGHTS TEMPERAMENT FACTOR

Effective sales competencies are the successful combination of behaviours, attitudes, values, emotional intelligencies, skills, and learned practices applied by top-performing sales professionals to deliver superior sales results. The SUCCESS INSIGHTS temperament factor (behaviours) is only one aspect of sales development.

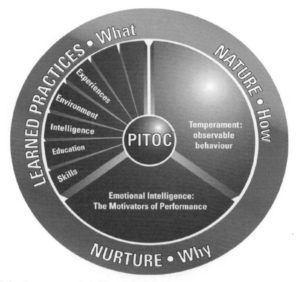

The Sales Competency Model™ provides a total framework to define, measure and develop the competencies of superior sales performance and allows critical sales competencies to be identified, learned and achieved.

The Sales Competency Model is made up of three components — three *natures* — of your total personality. Your *first nature* is temperament which is your inborn observable behaviours. It is 'how' you tend to do things. Your *second nature* is your motivators, beliefs, attitudes, values and emotional intelligencies. It is your nurture or the reasons 'why' you tend to do things. Your *third nature* is your learned practices which you have acquired formally or informally and which obviously have a huge impact on 'what' you do.

Your awareness, understanding and ability to integrate these three elements goes a long way towards maximising your overall sales competencies and you will find many of the root causes of sales mediocrity and poor performance in your *first nature* — the focus of this book.

Your core personal and professional sales competencies — who you are, what you do, how you do things — have their origins in your temperament profile more than any other personality factor. Understanding the power and benefits of this temperament language is, therefore, critically important to defining, measuring and developing your overall sales competency make-up.

THE UNIVERSAL TEMPERAMENT LANGUAGE
STRENGTHS [+] AND WEAKNESSES [–] OF THE FOUR
COLOURS

Temperament is your inborn observable natural behaviour. It affects your manner of acting, feeling, thinking and therefore selling. It is <u>how</u> you go about doing things. It is <u>how</u> you tend to communicate or approach a customer or a sales problem.

The Temperament Wheel shows the "natural" strengths and weaknesses of the four colour styles.

Have you been misjudged by another person? Have you ever had 'a personality clash' with a colleague, boss or customer? Have you ever met a customer and 'just clicked' from the word go? Have you ever questioned your own ability to do something? The answers to these questions may be closer to hand than you think.

The four colours — Red, Yellow, Green, Blue — match the four behaviour patterns described by William Molten Marston in 1928. Your boss, colleagues and customers are mapped somewhere on the Temperament Wheel and a clear knowledge of your own colour and especially that of your customer will greatly improve your ability to sell more products to more customers in less time and with less stress.

There is a direct correlation between your colour position and your 'affinity' with such vital skills of selling as: Prospecting, building rapport, qualifying, presenting, influencing, time management, closing, and follow-up. In other words, how you use, or do not use, the universal skills of selling will be profoundly affected by your <u>first nature</u> — your inborn behaviours. Some skills will come naturally to you, while others will require a 'conscious' learning effort.

How a Strength Over-used can be a Weakness or Stressful

Learning to sell with a higher 'awareness' level of your 'nature' can have an immense impact on your overall sales results. However, other personality and external factors can lead you to "overextend" your temperament style. In other words, a strength over-used can become a weakness. Awareness of your "over-extention" can help control this expression of your dominant colour – for the better.

BLUE
Tendency: To proceed cautiously
Over-extension: Questions too much
What causes stress: Surprises and unpredictability

RED
Tendency: To tell the customer what to do
Over-extension: Pushes too hard
What causes stress: Inefficiency and indecisiveness

GREEN
Tendency: Help resolve customer problems
Over-extension: Agrees too much
What causes stress: Insensitivity and impatience

YELLOW
Tendency: To interact easily
Over-extension: Talks too much
What causes stress: Boredom and Routine

The tendency to over use your strengths can work against you and even be stressful.

How does each colour react to stress?

Your first natural reaction to stressful situation will probably be the fuller expression of your dominant colour and in this sense a strength overused can become a weakness. In other words, Reds become more red, more direct (blunt); Greens become more patient (tolerant); Blues become more apprehensive (avoid); and Yellows become more expressive (indiscreet).

On the other hand, a weakness is often an undiscovered strength. Your shadow side (opposite colour) is a kind of 'splinter' or inferior part of your temperament which is often denied expression in everyday life. In fact, the attributes you reject most in others are often the direct personification of your shadow side — so honor all the colours in yourself and respect the difference in others. Carl Jung said: "The medicine we need is so always bitter".

Therefore, a good way to check your levels of stress is to ask yourself "How strongly you are using your primary colour?". The solution may be to pull back and "borrow" some of your opposite colour. For example, a Green tends to tolerate or agree even more than normal under stress. Whereas a stress reducer may be to consciously learn how to confront people and issues more quickly (Red behaviour).

DEVELOPING THE SUCCESS INSIGHTS SYSTEM FROM SIMPLICITY TO COMPLEXITY

The Success Insights system has several forms — "Wheels" — to help understand the complexity of human nature. Starting with the basic four colours to, the eight professional types, to 60 positions on the complete Success Insights™ wheel, to pinpoint accuracy in a computerised report. All these versions are designed to increase awareness and levels of understanding so that sales professionals can apply these lessons in their day-to-day work.

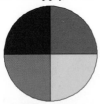

1. FROM 4 COLOURS STYLES

The four colours are a very powerful classification for behaviour analysis. However, everyone has their own unique configuration or blend of temperament style. So be careful not to stereotype someone as 'just' one of the colours! Remember also your 'colour' is only one clue to an understanding of your behaviour — your total sales personality is best viewed through The Sales Competency Model.

2. TO 8 PROFESSIONAL TYPES

The eight types are a professional classification to broaden your understanding of the Insights system. Each colour blends with its nearest neighbour to give four mixed colours (or types). Each of the eight names are an indicator (only) of that character. Each type should help further clarify your own "positioning" and your customer's type.

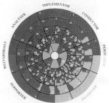

3. TO 60 POSITIONS

The Success Insights ™ wheel has 60 computerised positions. Each position is influenced by (1) Its dominant colour and which secondary colour influences it and (2) The distance from the centre of the wheel (the nearer the circumference the more intense the "nature").

4. TO MULTIPLE COLOURS

You are more than likely a mixture of the colours and this wheel shows the colour combination more clearly. In fact, only 5% of the population are one pure colour. Each of the eight types has seven or eight plot positions. In this form, you get even more detail and clarity about your temperament position.

5. TO A PERSONALISED COMPUTER REPORT

An individual computerised report can personalise your exact "uniqueness" with even more accuracy. There are 384 possible computerised reports and these have thousands of computerised variations. You are unique! You are complex. This, of course, is your definitive profiler because you have filled it out and only you know yourself well enough to complete such an exercise.

Your Unique Position on the Colour Wheel

You are unique! There is a 20 billion-to-one chance that there will be another individual exactly like you. On the Temperament Wheel, there are several thousand permutations possible from your computer report, which you can complete over the Internet. There are 384 standard reports and 60 positions (see below). The four colours, of course, give the broad view.

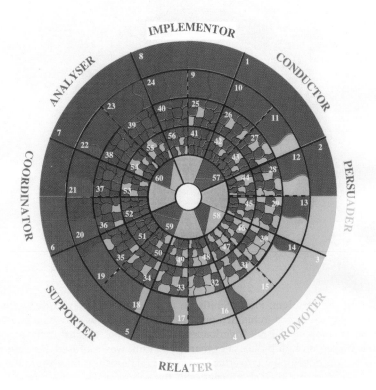

Your home base is one of these 60 positions and as you can see most positions have a mixture of colours. Hence the folly of labelling someone red, yellow, green or blue alone because most positions have two or three colours. Behavioural profiles as indicators of a skill are useful but not sufficient — they help us understand what a person is capable of doing, not what they will do.

Important! Be careful! Don't jump to conclusions. Temperament profiling is observing behaviour, only — it's what can be seen and heard. It's directly observable. Invisible qualities — values, attitudes — lie beneath the behavioural surface. Be careful not to misinterpret or "add meaning" to what you see and hear. In other words don't "contaminate" your observations with judgements or influences.

CASE STUDY: HONOUR THE DIFFERENCE

All sales competencies can be defined, measured and developed but their origins are firmly rooted in one of the four temperament styles. There is often a direct correlation between your Insights position and your superior functional/occupational sales competencies. Your behavioural disposition provides a panoramic insight into your competency set.

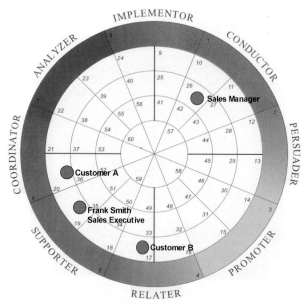

Defining the problem: Frank Smith, an experienced sales executive with a successful track record in his two previous companies, was only nine months in his new company. He felt "overloaded and drowning" because of the expectations placed on him by his sales manager. Frank was confused, because he knew he was developing two critical customer relationships that would transform his career and the sales revenues of the company. He felt a steady key account management approach was best. His sales manager wanted results and closure.

Measuring the people: We profiled the key players and two customers A & B on the Success Insights Wheel. Eureka! The opposite styles of the sales executive and the sales manager highlighted the difficulties between them. The clash of approaches was clear. Fortunately, both were mature listeners and willing to learn from the opposite styles.

Developing the solution: Both executives agreed to honour the difference between them and to stretch across the wheel to appreciate the strong points of the other. We tend to either judge ("they push our buttons") or over-value ("they can do no wrong") people whose primary profile position is in <u>our</u> shadow side. Beware of this! Both men agreed through sales coaching to look at the other person as their teacher. Two months later, customers A and B signed big contracts and justified the steadiness shown by the men.

HONOUR ALL THE COLOURS IN YOURSELF: UNCOVERING YOUR SHADOW SIDE

Everyone has a shadow side to their temperament. It is a kind of "splinter" or inferior part of your temperament that is often denied expression in everyday life. Your shadow is largely your opposite colour and to develop your personal competencies you may need to embrace your shadow side.

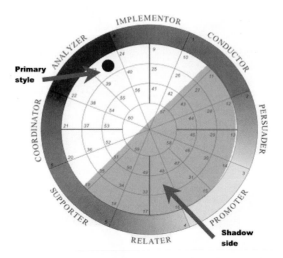

The attributes that you most reject in another person (things that irritate you) are often your shadow side seeking to express itself. It's your vulnerable side. It needs embracing and due attention. If you ignore your shadow side, it will frequently turn against you and manifest this rejection in the form of stress, illness and constant struggle with individuals whose primary position is in your shadow side.

Your challenge is to reclaim and rebuild these lost or ignored energies within yourself. **Honour all the colours within yourself ... then honour the difference in others**.

This allows you to develop "dormant" parts of your personality. *Carl Jung* defines the "whole person" as the self. And this is a big step in that direction.

THE LESSONS OF YOUR NATURE

Ultimately, everyone needs to sell ideas, products or themselves. Most people, however, are 'amateurs' in this vital competency. You can gain a professional edge by learning these four valuable lessons.

Sometimes one moment of insight is worth a lifetime of experience! Selling is a learnable competency that you can master. This book gives you the 'insights' and lessons on one vital aspect of human performance improvement that can change your life.

4:

HOW DOES YOUR CUSTOMER SEE YOU?

The Scottish poet, Robbie Burns, once said that "being able to see ourselves as others see us" is a great gift. Indeed, it is often the first step towards understanding ourselves.

But you are already a good way down the road towards greater awareness and self-knowledge! Knowing the impression you make on other people is an important step in the process of acquiring a more balanced image of yourself. Once you understand the impression you make in your communications with others, it is up to you to decide – consciously – whether to reinforce or lessen that effect. If you are fully aware how others see you, you can be more flexible in your own reactions towards them.

Of course, it is not possible to say with certainty what other people think of us. Some people are so convinced of themselves that the thought would never cross their minds that others might not find them as fantastic, as intelligent or as beautiful as they see themselves. But most people have a pretty good idea how other people might see them. More frequently, they tend to believe that other people do not like them, even though that is not the case at all.

The best way to find out how you seem to other people is to ask them. Of course, this does not mean shocking your customers with a clumsy "Well, how was I today?". Start with friends or colleagues who are well-disposed towards you and whose opinion you accept. First, consider what exactly you want to know. Now and again, ask one of your managers to accompany you to sales meetings, and collect some feedback. Ask them what you did well and where you could have been better. Collecting feedback does not mean listening only to negative comments but also reaping praise and recognition where they are deserved. You have to be familiar with both your strengths and your weaknesses.

The following checklist will help you to find out from others how they see you.

CHECKLIST: HOW DO I APPEAR?

What impression do I give when I arrive at the office in the morning?

When we talk, do you have the feeling that I understand you?

Do I allow you to express your opinion, or do I interrupt you frequently?

Does my body language express interest and a willingness to accommodate you, or does it convey a rejection?

Is it acceptable for you when I interrupt you, or does that disturb you?

Do I display a lot of emotion? How do you find that?

Do you find it easy to work with me? Why?

You will probably be able to find other questions connected with your work that will help you to find out how other people see you. However, never limit your "inquiries" to only one person. It might be that that particular person has a problem with certain character traits of yours, which others find perfectly acceptable. The best way to find out how you appear to others is to listen to many different opinions.

EXERCISE:
HOW YOU MIGHT APPEAR TO OTHERS

Of course, one of the most difficult things for other people is to give you negative feedback and for you, the most difficult thing is accepting it. This requires a relationship of trust, so be sure to ask only friends and colleagues who you know are not trying to get at you somehow and will not tell you things that are not true. Take your time in order to find out which things you do that rub others up the wrong way.

And do be self-critical. Observe yourself closely and see where other people have problems dealing with the way you act. That does not mean that the way you act is intrinsically wrong – it simply means that it irritates this particular person.

Decide which group of (admittedly not exactly flattering) traits fits your behaviour best.

BLUE	RED
CONSCIENTIOUS	**DOMINANT**
exact	dominating
analytical	controlling
critical	able to make decisions
detail-oriented	goal-oriented
distant	practical
STEADFAST	**TAKES THE INITIATIVE**
steady	flamboyant
a creature of habit	open-minded
needs security	optimistic
understanding	enthusiastic
reliable	creative
GREEN	YELLOW

1. Which segment of the wheel describes you best? Even if you think that several might fit, which is usually the case, choose just one.

2. In this vague perception of how others might see you, is there one word that you recognise as apt but which you would like to eradicate from your image of your personality? Which word?
3. Why?
4. Which adjective in the segment of the wheel you chose would you say definitely describes one of your personal weaknesses?
5. Is there an adjective in the segment you chose which does not apply to you at all? Which one?

Which colour type description fits you best?
In private life?   _____
In professional life?   _____

Were you able to identify more closely with one segment of the wheel? There is no need to be ashamed of your negative characteristics. Everyone is bad-tempered or stubborn or incorrect at one time or another.

After all, you display the negative characteristics in "your" segment of the wheel only on a bad day. Or is that perhaps not true? Or could it be that some people find this behaviour, perhaps in a milder form, typical for you even on a good day? Of course, this is not only influenced by the way you are, but by their disposition also. Usually, the people who have most difficulty accepting your characteristics will be those whose segment lies exactly opposite yours. They are more inclined to take a negative view of you, on a good or a bad day.

**EXERCISE:
LOOKING AT YOUR STRENGTHS AND
WEAKNESSES THROUGH VARIOUS GLASSES**

Think about what you yourself would consider your strengths
and weaknesses. Then consider what others see as your
strong and weak points. Perhaps you have talked about this
with friends before. If not, perhaps you could ask now.

	Your strengths	**Your weaknesses**
As you see them		
As the others see them		

When you ask about your strengths and weaknesses, do you
get the same answers from everyone?
Ask colleagues to draw up a similar list and compare your
strengths and weaknesses. Perhaps this will help you see why
other people see particular characteristics of yours as
strengths or weaknesses.

Imagine the following situation: An insurance company holds its
annual sales conference for its best and most successful insurance
sales consultants. This year, the sales consultant with the highest
sales is the quiet, more introverted John Hall. Steve Jones, a
journalist working in local radio, would like to interview him. He
finds John Hall's sales figures extremely impressive and asks a
thousand questions about the secret of his success. "Is Mr Hall
excited about his success, and what do his colleagues think about
it?" But John Hall is very uncommunicative. He sits in front of
Steve Jones, arms folded, and eyes the microphone suspiciously.
His answers are brief, offhand and his voice monotone. For Jones,
it seems unimaginable that this dry character should be such a
successful insurance salesperson.

Do you know what colour types John Hall and Steve Jones are?
You probably guessed: John Hall has strong Blue elements in his
make-up – perfectly suited to the job of an insurance sales

consultant, where he can take the time he needs to put together offers that are tailor-made to his customers' requirements. He probably also has strong Green aspects – he understands his customers' desire for security, and they trust him. However, if he is put under pressure, as in our interview situation, and a Yellow type like Steve Jones jumps on him with a thousand different questions, he withdraws into his shell, becomes suspicious and indifferent. If Steve Jones had been aware of this, he would have allowed John Hall plenty of time to gain confidence in him, would have explained to him beforehand what questions he was thinking of asking, and John Hall would have known what was expected of him. However, as things were, the interview was doomed to failure. And Steve Jones went home with a completely different picture of John Hall as a sales professional from the one that John Hall's customers have.

How you appear to others depends on:

- The way you act
- Your customer's style
- The situation.

Finally, we would like to offer you a checklist that might give you some ideas on how to ask your customer how they see you. Make your questions as concrete as possible, so that you will get concrete answers. And only ask your questions if there is an atmosphere of trust. Remember: A Yellow will answer your questions readily and thinks it is a good idea of yours to ask them. A Red customer might become impatient and take the opportunity to annoy you a little. So remember who you are asking these questions and consider whether you can expect an honest answer. However, do not assume that a Red customer will not give you any honest answers – they will, but perhaps only to one or two questions and not to the whole list.

CHECKLIST: HOW DID IT GO?

Before the presentation: "What do you know already about my product?"

During the presentation: "Just let me know if anything is not quite clear. I'd be happy to explain it to you."

After your meeting: "Are you satisfied with the way the meeting went?"

"I would like to prepare myself as well as possible for our next meeting. What do you need from me next time in addition to what we have already discussed?" "Is there anything you felt I left out this time?"

"Would you like us to meet in the same place? Or would you prefer to meet in my office or in a restaurant?"

"Are there any points which need clarification? Did you like my presentation? Or did you feel it lacked something?"

"Your feedback is important to me. I would like to know how you found my presentation.'

"I felt our meeting was very pleasant, and I'm leaving you with a good feeling. How about you? Is there anything we need to clarify?"

"I get the feeling you were not quite happy with our meeting. Is that right?"

"What can I do to ensure that we are both satisfied with the outcome of our meeting?"

"Unfortunately, I wasn't able to accommodate your wishes this time. I hope you understand the reasons behind this. Or is there anything we need to clarify?"

5:

HOW DO YOU SELL TO YOUR CUSTOMERS?

Now let us take a look at your selling style. In this chapter, you can check whether your estimate of which colour group you belong to has been right so far, or whether you need to look in a different direction. The detailed portrayals of the different selling styles of the four colour groups will give you a clear idea of where your strengths and weaknesses are as a salesperson. It will also show you the strengths of the other colour styles. You may perhaps like to integrate aspects of them into your own selling style.

First, however, here are two exercises that offer you the chance to analyse more closely the way you sell.

EXERCISE:
ANALYSING YOUR SELLING STYLE

1. Are you self-confident?
2. Do you try to close a deal quickly?
3. Do you try to use your authority as a salesperson and an expert to convince your customers?
4. Do you prefer selling new and innovative products?
5. Do details bore you, so that you only explain the "most important" points?
6. Do you enjoy jokes and small talk?

---

7. Do you enjoy winning new customers?
8. Are you often pushed for time because you spend too much time with one customer?
9. Do you enjoy providing extra services for your longstanding customers?
10. Do you rarely put your customers under pressure to buy?
11. Do you prefer selling products you yourself are enthusiastic about?
12. Do you ask a lot of questions in order to find out exactly what your customer wants?
13. Do you enjoy discussing details?
14. Do you spend a lot of time working with facts and figures?
15. Do you come straight to the point and not waste time with small talk?
16. Have you always got written material prepared for your customers?

Evaluation:
If you answered "Yes" to the following questions, your selling style tends to be in the following direction:

Questions 1 to 4:   Red
Questions 5 to 8:   Yellow
Questions 9 to 12:   Green
Questions 13 to 16:   Blue

Your basic attitude to your customer is a good indicator of which style suits you. Think about which of these attitudes is more characteristic for you.

EXERCISE:
RECOGNISING YOUR BASIC ATTITUDE AS A
SALES PROFESSIONAL

Basic Attitude   **My Style   Not My Style**

1. "There is only one way to sell
    something: Treat your customer
    very seriously and move quickly."
2. "Concentrate on making yourself
    popular, and the deal will take
    care of itself."
3. "Don't try to force it. You can't
    do much to influence a customer
    anyway. Just be ready and waiting
    with a pen and an order form
    when the customer is ready to
    place his order."
4. "I let my facts and the information
    speak for me. If it is logical and
    the ideal solution, the customer
    will be clever enough to recognise
    it. I just provide him with the data."

Evaluation:
You have probably already recognised which basic attitude
corresponds to which colour style:
Basic attitude 1:   Red salesperson
Basic attitude 2:   Yellow salesperson
Basic attitude 3:   Green salesperson
Basic attitude 4:   Blue salesperson

Which colour style fits your attitude to selling?

What is Your Selling Style?

Below, you will find descriptions of the typical behaviour patterns of salespeople of the four colour groups. While you read the outlines, compare the descriptions with your own selling style. Make notes, and underline key words or phrases that you can recognise in your own work.

Now you can go one step further and find out whether you are a mixed style and, if so, a mixture of which styles. You will also remember the eight professional temperament types. Of course, you will not be able to say whether you are a cross-type X or perhaps the more flexible type Y. This is not possible. Leave such detailed analysis to a computer. But you will find hints of where your selling style contains elements of two or three overlapping colour styles.

Bearing these thoughts in mind, go through the outlines. Talk to friends and colleagues about your personal selling style and how others see it. Every style has its weak points, but do not let that deter you. Even if you identify with a particular style, you do not have to display every weakness (or strength) of that style. Not everything applies to everyone. And already, consciously or unconsciously, you may have learned to compensate for a natural weakness with a natural strength, because your job demanded it.

Are You a Red Salesperson?

Basic attitude

"The fastest way to close the sale is to tell the customer what they need to know in short, clear and convincing arguments."

How you approach sales meetings with customers

You see the customer and, within a matter of seconds, you know what they need. You would like to prove to them that you are an expert, so first of all you tell them everything they need to know about the product. Brief inquiries are enough to tell you exactly what the customer wants, and this is exactly what you offer them with the help of short, clear and convincing arguments. Sometimes the claims you make are a little exaggerated, especially when you notice that the customer is not quite convinced by what you are explaining. Nevertheless, your presentation is very persuasive and emphatic and leaves a good impression.

Unfortunately, in all of this you sometimes forget to check with customers whether this really is what they want. In many cases, you are perfectly right, but sometimes you can browbeat customers with your authoritarian manner. Some customers are too timid to contradict openly, and you may not notice that you are barking up the wrong tree. You may be afraid of losing control of the meeting if your customer gets the chance to talk for too long.

Once you have told them all they need to know about the product, you may name your price and delivery periods and push the customer to close the sale there and then.

Your attitude to the customer

You may not really deem it necessary to establish a relationship of trust with the customer. It is a waste of time: first, because other customers are waiting for you and, second, because you already know what your customer needs anyway. So you may think lengthy discussions with customers are superfluous.

You expect the customer to believe what you tell them – you know that you have got your facts right. You already know what objections your customer will raise and you take the wind out of their sails by presenting the corresponding arguments to disarm them. You simply knock down any other arguments the customer might present. In fact, your motto is "Knock all objections down before they knock you down." But, even if you don't see it, you run the risk of not noticing that many customers feel completely browbeaten by all your facts and arguments.

Closing the deal

You close the deal without much fuss. If you don't land it at the first meeting, you go on to the second and so on, refusing to give up until the customer gives in. Closing a deal is a test of strength for you – one that you win by overcoming the customer's resistance and objections.

Your strengths

- Your self-confidence and your single-mindedness give you the ideal air of authority, and people see you as an expert. You are not afraid of approaching any customer. You even enjoy taking a crack at difficult customers – you like the challenge.
- You are good at judging situations and your questions usually give the meeting a nudge in the right direction.
- During your presentation, you brilliantly sum up all the individual points without forgetting any important details or wasting time unnecessarily.
- You present a solution very convincingly. If you inquire, you can often come up with apt, suitable options that can help your customer make up their mind. You immediately obtain written confirmation of the order.
- You can offer excellent follow-up – but only from those customers high up on your priority list and those you expect substantial orders from in the future.

Your weaknesses

- Your style may appear pushy and exaggerated to others. Many of your customers could feel browbeaten. You may like to use fear as a form of motivation.
- You often get to the core of things too quickly and do not take enough time to establish a relationship with the customer. Some see your air of self-confidence as arrogance.
- You often fail to listen to what your customers have to say or you interrupt them. You do not react when they ask questions or you answer them straight away without considering their

arguments. Customers have the feeling that you are only waiting for them to stop talking to draw breath, and then you will jump in and take over the conversation again. In particular, your presentation is too hurried. You assume that your customer will understand everything immediately. If they do not, you can become impatient. Customers may feel threatened by the whole situation and feel they are being coerced into making a decision before they are ready to do so.

- Often, this means that many of your customers will later withdraw their orders. The moment you walk out the door, your customers may regret the decision you pressurised them into making and are likely to cancel the order.

- If a customer is no longer a challenge for you, or bores you with routine requests, you can lose interest in them quickly. You may let the deal fall through or become lax in your follow-up.

ARE YOU A YELLOW SALESPERSON?

Basic attitude

"If I create a friendly atmosphere and build a friendly relationship, the customer will like me, which will make it easier to pull off the deal in the end."

How you approach sales meetings with customers

You start off with relaxed small talk, ask how the customer is, chat about this and that or tell a few amusing anecdotes. You are in no hurry to get down to business. It is important first to give the customer the feeling that you are their friend. Nothing could be further from your mind than pushing them or taking them by surprise. Your tone is warm and pleasant, even if you do not know your customer very well yet.

And when you start your presentation, your conversational tone hardly changes. You speak informally, in a relaxed manner, and the product itself is not necessarily your central subject. Your presentation is more unstructured, rambling; often, you do not have a concrete plan in your mind.

Your attitude to the customer

The most important thing for you is to establish a good atmosphere and a friendly relationship, because you believe this is good for getting sales. However, building up trust does not seem as important to you. You want to keep the conversation going – then you will find out what your customer needs.

If your customers raise objections, you agree with them, side-step the issues or change the subject. If you can avoid it, you do not like to talk about things that could disturb your relationships with your customers.

Closing the deal

You will not hurry your customers. If they want to buy, sooner or later they will be ready to close the deal. But you often find an amusing way to persuade them to sign the contract.

Your strengths

- Winning new customers is one of the areas where you come into your own. You enjoy contacting new people. For you, everyone is a potential customer.
- Your laid-back, self-confident style relaxes most customers. You approach them with a positive attitude and a friendly manner.
- You are imaginative, adaptable and flexible. It is easy for you to ask spontaneous questions that will provide you with useful information on your customer's requirements.
- You enjoy your own entertaining presentation and make every effort to make it entertaining for your customer. Your enthusiasm for a creative solution is infectious.

- The sales negotiations end on a light, relaxed note, and your closing of the deal is often very imaginative.
- Your follow-up is very creative and sociable.

Your weaknesses

- Your preparation is often hurried and insufficient, and does not meet the customer's requirements. If you take a too relaxed attitude here, you may lose the deal.
- Sometimes the fact that you skimped on your preparation means that you can ask only superficial or unrealistic questions, particularly on complex subjects. You tend to leave one subject hanging in mid-air while you rush on to the next.
- You get carried away easily, wander off the subject, exaggerate and sometimes seem almost a caricature. Sometimes you do not listen to what your customer has to say and do not have the patience to clarify all the details.
- You tend to lose interest after the initial rush, when routine takes over or when the whole thing becomes too complicated.
- You believe that your customer will buy from you if they like you – and over and over again, you will see that this is a false conclusion.

ARE YOU A GREEN SALESPERSON?

Basic attitude

"You can't really force or influence a deal. Inevitably, it is up to the customer to make up their own mind. All you can do is take an order when the customer is ready."

How you approach sales meetings with customers

Pushing yourself into the limelight or dictating the tone is not your style. Your presentation is factual, but somewhat colourless, especially if you are unable to identify yourself with the product. You simply describe the product, and then you feel it is up to your customer to make up their mind. You will not try unduly to influence them. However, if customers have questions, or describe what they are looking for, you listen attentively and are at pains to provide them with a solution. You take time to ask as many questions as necessary until you know exactly what they want, although it is often the customer who takes the initiative.

Your attitude to the customer

Under no circumstances do you want to crowd your customer, and so you remain aloof. You do not believe that trust can be established in such a short period of time anyway. On the other hand, when you have known a customer for a long time, you open up and warm up.

You sometimes ignore objections or simply accept them. You know as well as the customer that every product has its disadvantage, and arguing could cause tension.

Closing the deal

It follows that the closing of the deal is often left open, if the customer is still undecided as to whether to buy. Your motto is: "The customer will tell me when they are ready to buy. I can wait ..." And, if the deal falls through, you think: "Oh, well. Better luck next time."

Your strengths

- Building long-term customer relationships is your natural competency. You can build up warm and lasting relationships on a close personal level. You are usually good at breaking the ice quickly and forging links with customers.

- You have the gift of being a natural listener, and you possess a great degree of sensitivity and the persistence to tackle the real problems. You are very good at analysing exactly what the customer wants and what you can offer them.
- Your presentation is based on your own personal values and ideals and will therefore be convincing and consistent.
- You close the deal sincerely and warmly.
- You are highly motivated to provide good and thorough follow-up, as you are sincerely interested in strengthening your business relationship.

Your weaknesses

- You may not like entering new prospecting situations. When you do, you first have to re-establish your image as a relator, and this requires great self-confidence. It takes quite an effort to behave like an expert. You may stiffen inwardly and your customer may notice this conflict and your unnatural behaviour.
- Sometimes you show off your personal moral concepts too much and these conflict with your customer's own values.
- Your presentation may lack enthusiasm and flair when you no longer feel on safe ground. Unexpected events could throw you off-track. The thought of delivering a presentation to a group of people gives you nightmares.
- You might hesitate to close a deal in order to avoid rejection. The last thing you want is to pressurise your customer, to make them feel uncomfortable or hurt their feelings.
- Should problems occur in after-sales follow-up, you are not particularly keen on facing them. You may not see them as a challenge but as a nuisance.

Can you see yourself in this situation: Two Green salespeople meet for a beer one evening. One says to the other: "Hey, I had a lot of interesting sales meetings today." The other answers: "I know. I didn't sell much either."

ARE YOU A BLUE SALESPERSON?

Basic attitude

"If I know everything about the product and the market, I'll be successful."

How you approach sales meetings with customers

You approach your customers with a friendly but reserved manner. You would like to sell them something but you do not want to establish contact on a personal level. You do not want to waste your time or theirs with small talk, so you come straight to the point. You are serious and formal.

Your presentation is slow-paced and well-structured but sometimes very dry. You allow your customer time to digest all the information. You are very practical-minded and ask questions. If the customer wants more details or technical information, you have written information to read later. You always have some with you, true to your motto: "If the customer has all the facts and options concerning our product, they will appreciate its high quality." And so you provide them with proof from reliable sources.

Your attitude to the customer

With great determination, you set about finding out about the customer's requirements. You encourage the customer to ask questions about your product, because you know that you are well-prepared to answer them. You have already gone through all possible objections in your mind and know how to disarm them. If there are still objections, you simply start all over again. Or you withdraw, interpreting the customer's objections as a signal that he needs more time to think about it. You offer to give him all alternatives and options in writing.

Closing the deal

You are very cautious and slow to close the deal. Once you have provided customers with all information they need on the product, it is up to them to make up their mind.

Your strengths

- Providing information. You are a real expert in this field, and it shows.
- You are extremely well-prepared for your first contact with a new customer. You have already gathered all available details about the customer.
- You are the master of the probing question that strikes to the very core of the problem.
- You are a good listener and sincerely interested in understanding your customer and finding out more about their company and its requirements.
- You are a walking data-bank, full of encyclopaedic knowledge about your product. In your presentations, you pay attention to every detail. You have all the information about every option right at your fingertips.
- You can analyse the customer's position precisely and evaluate the facts thoroughly. Your follow-up is exemplary, and your next visit will be just as perfectly planned as this one.

Your weaknesses

- Your welcome can be somewhat stiff. You appear quiet and reticent, which can hamper relationship-building. Building rapport and small talk are not your strong points.
- Some people find your insistent questions pushy, critical and tactless.
- Sometimes you cannot see the wood for the trees. You are fascinated by the details and can thus lose sight of your goal. In this way, you may fail to appreciate your customer's true needs and wishes.

- There is more to good customer contact than just providing the facts. After a sales meeting with you, some customers may not be keen to see you again because they found the whole thing too impersonal and too strenuous.

Think about the profiles of the selling styles for the four colours again: Which style can you identify most with? Which style bears the greatest resemblance to your selling style? Which styles is it impossible for you to identify with at all?

WHERE ARE YOUR STRENGTHS AS A SALES PROFESSIONAL?

If you know your own strengths, then you are also aware of your weaknesses. The following exercises give you the chance to take a more in-depth look at your strong points. Do not be too modest about them. Every top sales professional should know their strengths and attributes and put them to work far more consciously.

The four stages of a sale

Frank Murphy is a car salesperson. He is quite ambitious, and because his commission is profit-linked, he is interested in closing deals quickly. At the outset of his career, he quickly established a certain reputation in his showrooms: people saw him as an aggressive salesperson. He was very good at convincing people. He was a real motor expert and hardly ever gave his customers a chance to contradict him. As he was also quite intelligent, he quickly got to know the typical arguments customers came up with and he disarmed them one by one in his presentation. He pointed out to his customers on most occasions that he was making them a unique offer that they really should take advantage of straightaway. And many of them were impressed and bought.

However, about one-third of them would withdraw from the deal within a few days. After a while, Frank became very frustrated with this pattern. Luckily, he had good colleagues who explained what he was doing wrong. They pointed out that he had had his sights fixed too firmly on closing the sale.

As a Red type, he was good at convincing people and he wanted results. His customers, half-persuaded and half-intimidated, agreed to buy. But there was a low level of trust between the two parties. The customers agreed with Frank Murphy as a salesperson at the moment of the sale but, in reality, they had no confidence in Frank Murphy the person. Hardly surprising – he rarely said anything personal to them or asked them about **their** wishes. When they got home, many of them felt they had been cheated and withdrew from the purchase.

One day, a sales trainer showed Frank an inverted pyramid outlining the four stages of a sale. He explained to Frank that studies had shown that each phase of a sale was important, but that the four stages were not equally important to the customer.

The sales trainer explained: "You have got as much as 40% of the sales task completed if you have established a basis of trust with your customer. A further 30% is achieved by means of an accurate and detailed needs analysis. Your presentation accounts for 20%. And only 10% depends on the closing offer you make the customer to close the deal. And, Frank, **your** chances drop to 70% from the outset, because you leave out the first two phases more or less completely."

Perhaps you are also familiar with the four stages of a professional sale (**Figure 5**). The percentages show the importance of each stage for the overall sales presentation to be a success.

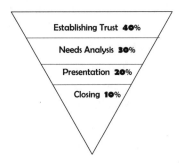

Figure 5: The four stages of a professional sale

This feedback was significant enough to persuade Frank Murphy to change his selling approach. He devoted far more time and energy to the first two stages and was then able to close most deals with the help of his convincing presentations, which clearly pointed out customer benefits. As a result, the number of customers withdrawing from sales deals fell to about 2% and his commission rose sharply.

EXERCISE:
REMEMBER SALES NEGOTIATIONS YOU HAVE CONDUCTED RECENTLY

Which stage of a sale are you best at?
What are your strengths in this stage?
Which stage are you weakest in?
Why? Where are the difficulties for you?

Our example has already shown the stage the Red excels in: in closing the deal. Establishing an atmosphere of trust is more the forte of the Green and Yellow colour styles, the Blues are likely to be better at needs analysis and the Yellows at making presentations. This is where their natural strengths lie.

And it follows that, in the other stages of the sale, where they are not so strong, they have to work harder to make the deal a success. Of course, this does not mean that, if you are a Yellow type, you will not be able to close the deal. But it does mean that you have a tendency not to approach the final phase directly enough, not demanding a clear answer from your customer.

The example also shows one thing clearly: A strength taken too far becomes a weakness. Frank Murphy was concentrating too hard on his natural strengths, which was closing deals, and the end result was the opposite of what he wanted.

Here's how you can check whether you have a tendency to push your strengths too far.

WHEN A STRENGTH BECOMES A WEAKNESS

Red

Your strength becomes a weakness:

- When you believe that customers always have problems making up their minds and that you will always have to push them to make a choice.
- When you solve conflicts with customers according to the motto "Argue first, and ask questions later".
- When your reaction to a dispute with a colleague is to shout at them. Later, you notice that hardly anyone speaks to you for the rest of the day.
- When you want to win at all costs, even in a training game.

Yellow

Your strength becomes a weakness:

- When you invite your toughest competitor to your Christmas Party.
- When you think everyone else is chaotic, but that you yourself are well-organised.
- When you convince yourself that you can persuade your customers to buy in the course of just one meeting.
- When you take it for granted that every customer likes you.

Green

Your strength becomes a weakness:

- When you spend all week slogging over a normal presentation, just to make sure you don't make any mistakes the customer could hold against you.
- When a customer raises an objection, you ask a question, ask another question and then wonder whether you should discuss it or not.
- When you realise that for the last 20 years, you have been playing golf with the same customers at the same time on the same day every week.

Blue

Your strength becomes a weakness:

- When you deliberately drive your car down to the very last drop of petrol so that you can measure its petrol consumption precisely.
- When you go shopping on the weekend wearing a suit and a tie.
- When you catch yourself phoning a customer because you have found a typing error in some of the written material you gave him.
- When you realise that you have a log of your golf scores on every hole for the last three months.

Which of these strengths turned into weaknesses seems most like you? Which of these weaknesses seems furthest from you?

CONCLUSION

Take stock. Which colour style was your behaviour characteristic of in all these exercises? If in doubt, remember that you could be a mixed style.

6:

WHAT STYLE IS YOUR CUSTOMER?

You are negotiating with a customer who displays many Yellow characteristics: They are enthusiastic about your presentation, friendly and obliging, they tell you a few amusing stories and talk quite a lot. But there are also a few characteristics that do not fit the typical Yellow. Your customer is also quite orderly, the documents on their desk are in neat piles, and they ask lots of questions until they are certain that they have understood your proposition. And they seem to have no problems making up their mind to buy your product. Such meticulousness and determination are not typical of the Yellow!

Which brings us to the subject of mixed styles. This customer displays many of the characteristics of the Yellow style, but also has Red traits: They can make up their mind and they require exact, precise information to help them make the right choice. They fit the picture of the Persuader.

It is possible to display characteristics of all four colour styles. As a rule, almost everyone displays strong characteristics of two, if not three, colour styles. These blends greatly determine how you behave. To make it easier for you to assess the way your customers act and to recognise mixed styles, we will introduce you to the eight main types in this chapter: four pure styles and four mixed styles. The mixed styles result from a blend of the characteristics of two neighbouring colour styles, Red-Yellow or

Green-Blue, for example. The eight types are explained in greater detail and described in relation to your occupation of selling.

We also describe the styles with which the eight types are most likely to experience problems, in order to illustrate that conflict often arises because two people are of opposite types. It is easier to be tolerant towards people who share the same rough edges as yourself, but far more difficult to be as understanding towards people who are completely different.

Often these people reflect our own deep-rooted fears: A Red customer, for example, might be on the defensive against a Green salesperson's need to establish a business relationship based on trust, because they themselves fear getting too close to others. This has very little to do with the Green salesperson's personality, but a Green salesperson may feel that the Red customer is rejecting them and may take it personally.

However, if the Red customer faces up to their fears, they can define their limits and protect themselves and, as a consequence, will no longer feel the need to brusquely reject the Green's need for a basis of trust. And *vice versa*: If the Green is aware that a Red customer does not feel the need for a relationship of trust, but wants to get to the business in hand quickly and in a businesslike manner, then they will no longer take the customer's rejection personally.

The tables listing the aims, methods, strengths, weaknesses, positive and negative impressions on others and the fears of each style provide an overview, not only of the strong, but also the critical, points for each type.

THE CONDUCTOR

The Conductor is definitely a Red type. As customers, they are

very straightforward, move with the times and are committed to their goals. They want to make a difference, to achieve important things. They do not like spending time on trifling deals, but prefer to negotiate large-scale projects where a lot of money is involved. They do not enjoy routine tasks or defining the minor details once the broad framework has been dealt with. But, nonetheless, they will perform these tasks, because they do not want to make any mistakes.

They enjoy making decisions and are often very demanding. They may seem cool, curt and arrogant. They solve problems logically and astutely. Single-mindedly, a Conductor will demand the information they need, not caring whether they interrupt you or disturb the flow of your sales presentation. Considering how others might feel is not their strong point – they think only of the information they need and their goals. They tend to overstep limits and often fail to treat other people with the respect due to them, while nevertheless expecting others to respect them. If you are disrespectful or too laid-back, they are likely to put you in your place in no uncertain terms.

Conductors set high standards for themselves – and everyone else. They are critical and quick to notice if other people make mistakes. If you give contradictory information during the meeting, they are sure to spot it. They will nail you down on this one point, and hold you to those terms that are most favourable to them. For the whole time you are with them, you will know for sure that it is the Conductor who is dictating the terms and that you can either accept their conditions or forget the deal. However, they will respect you if you are a tough negotiator and refuse to give way on points that are important to you, standing your ground just as stubbornly as they do. They do not like personal criticism but ironically they will always try to put the blame on you if something goes wrong.

A Conductor is the kind of customer with whom you can close a deal in the shortest amount of time. If you are well-prepared and present them with the information they require without delay, if you are credible and self-confident and have some real product/service advantages to tempt them with, they will not waste much time before accepting your offer.

The Conductor

Goal	Dominance, independence, change, results
Methods	Quick, determined, astute, can be inconsiderate
Strengths	Leadership qualities, enthusiasm, perseveres until succeeds, has a gift for getting people to achieve a desired result
Weaknesses	Impatient, argumentative, egocentric
Negative impression	Arrogant, hard, critical
Positive impression	Self-assured, a leader, bold, a strong character
Fears	Routine, loss of control, getting too close

The Conductor is most likely to have problems with salespeople from these styles:

- *Relator*: The Green-Yellow Relator is too understanding. The Conductor finds this unimportant. They do not know what to think of the Relator's helpfulness, since they seldom ask for help themselves. Instead, they simply demand what they require. The Conductor feels little respect for a Green-Yellow salesperson – in their eyes, they are laying themselves open to exploitation. They find it very difficult to strike the intimate tone the Relator would like. When the Relator gives them advice, for example suggests that they should take advantage of this or that special service, it is very hard for the Conductor to accept it. They do not like advice – after all, they know exactly what they want.

- *Supporter*: From the Conductor's point of view, a salesperson who is a Green/Supporter may not offer sufficiently innovative products or flexible solutions. The Supporter likes as little change as possible, while the Conductor needs flexibility and new and better products, so conflict is inevitable. The Conductor does not want the tried and tested, they like to experiment with new things if they promise higher productivity. In addition, they will be irritated by the fact that the Supporter does not offer them sufficient resistance and will not enter into tough negotiations. The Supporter adapts too readily to suit the person they are negotiating with and always reacts in the same friendly manner, whatever happens. The Conductor is the opposite – they refuse to adapt and readily show their displeasure.
- *Co-ordinator*: The Conductor often has no answers to the logical arguments presented by a salesperson who is a Green-Blue Co-ordinator. But this does not mean that these arguments will persuade them to abandon their pre-formed opinions. The Conductor would like to argue with the Co-ordinator about conditions, about the price or delivery periods, but the Co-ordinator will not argue. The Co-ordinator wants to discuss these things, and does not mind at all if the meeting drags on – as long as it is fair. In turn, this endless discussion gets on the Conductor's nerves, but the anger and pressure that are their preferred tools have no effect on the Co-ordinator. They firmly reject the Conductor's personal aggression.

THE PERSUADER

The Persuader is the Red-Yellow mixed style. As a customer,

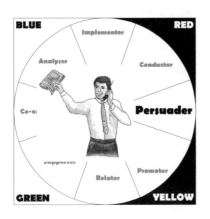

results are just as important as personal relationships. They are pleasant partners to negotiate with because, while they are prepared to exchange a few personal words, they never lose sight of the business in hand. They want to make their own decisions and are always keen to gain recognition and to move up the career ladder. That is why you can persuade them to participate in a risky or absolutely new business venture. However, in spite of having one eye on their career and personal prestige, they still want to be popular and respected. When making decisions, they consider other people's interests. If they are forced to make unpopular decisions, they will try to find the best possible solution for all concerned. They will not strike you from their list just because they have found someone who quotes them a lower price. But they will expect you to accommodate them and to make them an offer acceptable to both sides.

They may like to involve their staff in the sales decision. When it comes to negotiating the details of a contract, they may leave it to a member of staff, but they will be supervising the decisions in the background. However, they are sometimes too optimistic in their assessment of what others can do. They do not like dealing with the finicky details of a contract themselves, but they will put up with it if it helps to achieve a specific goal. They need variety and love to jet around the world. They know lots of people with whom they maintain good, friendly contacts. To other people, they seem dynamic and enthusiastic, though some people will find Persuaders rash and indiscreet.

The Persuader

Goal	Power, position, recognition, achieving results through others
Methods	Convincing others, passing on enthusiasm, inspiring others to achieve
Strengths	Optimistic, gregarious, strong-willed
Weaknesses	Craves admiration, too trusting
Negative impression	Shallow, talkative, indiscreet
Positive impression	Enthusiastic, happy, motivating
Fears	Failure, loss of responsibility

The Persuader is most likely to have problems with salespeople of these types:

- *Supporter:* The Green salesperson mainly offers them tried and tested products, and that is not what the Persuader is looking for. They cannot win any laurels with those. To the Persuader, the Supporter's retiring manner appears boring. They want to get enthusiastic about a product, not just hear why it is so reliable. The Persuader has great difficulty understanding the Supporter's need for security.

- *Co-ordinator*: The Blue-Green salesperson is very correct and thus the exact opposite of the Persuader. All their grand ideas burst like so many bubbles against the Co-ordinator's precise analyses. The Persuader is not so fond of logical arguments that bring them back down-to-earth. They prefer a salesperson who thinks above and beyond the conventional and who will come up with a new and individual solution especially for them.

- *Analyser*: The same thing happens with the Blue salesperson. They judge things with their head and refuse to get carried away with the Persuader's grandiose ideas. Moreover, the Analyser is very reserved and there is little real connection between them and the Persuader. The Persuader prefers customers with whom they can chat about personal subjects and who will play with ideas with them. They do appreciate the precise information the Blue salesperson provides, but on the whole, they find them too "dry".

THE PROMOTER

The Promoter is the bright Yellow style who needs to surround

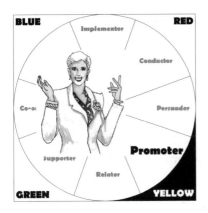

themselves with other people. They have a huge network of contacts at their disposal. Their natural eloquence enables them to sell themselves and their ideas very well. However, sometimes they may over-estimate the effect they have on others and their own talents. Creativity is the Promoter's great strength. However, putting their creative ideas into action may be their greatest weakness. The Promoter may not be natural leadership material, because they are not consistent or authoritarian enough. Their desire to get on well with others is greater than their desire to lead them.

They often get into difficulties with their various tasks and time schedules and chaos takes over. It is not easy to give a flowing presentation to a Promoter – they are constantly interrupting. The Promoter wants the salesperson to take up their ideas and expects sales talks to be more lively discussion than tough negotiations. If they are not sure, they will hesitate to make a decision, but they will not openly admit that they are not convinced.

The Promoter

Goal	Popularity, confirmation, inspiring ideas
Method	Spontaneous, enthusiastic, volatile
Strengths	Can inspire others, relieve tension, support others, is eloquent
Weaknesses	Is often unreliable, especially where time-planning is concerned, is unorganised and unrealistic
Negative impression	Superficial, flattering, volatile
Positive impression	Motivating, , sunny, inspiring
Fears	Loss of self-esteem and social recognition, isolation

The Promoter is most likely to have problems with salespeople of these styles:

- *Analyser*: These two are like chalk and cheese. The Blue salesperson is absolutely precise in everything they do. They think everything through, right down to the very last detail, whereas the Promoter has flashes of creative inspiration with which they like to motivate themselves and others. When the Analyser tries to convince them of the advantages of a product, using a multitude of facts and details to support their arguments, the Promoter is bored to tears. They need images and visuals and must be able to imagine how something works. The Analyser, on the other hand, will try to win them over with logic and systematic arguments, which makes no impression whatsoever on the Promoter.

- *Co-ordinator*: Blue-Green salespeople also tend to make their presentation very informative, but not particularly lively. They offer tried and tested products, but these rarely correspond to the Promoter's innovative ideas. The Co-ordinator is also easily thrown off track when the Promoter frequently interrupts their presentation, spends a lot of the time talking themselves and jumps from one subject to another.

- *Implementor*: The Red-Blue salesperson is striving for perfection and outstanding results and proceeds cautiously and logically. They, too, will have problems with the speed with which the Promoter jumps from one subject to the next. They can appreciate that the Promoter wants new products and innovative solutions but, to their way of thinking, the Promoter does not give ideas due consideration before acting, and so they have problems respecting a Yellow customer. And the Promoter, in turn, cannot get on with what they see as the Implementor's pernickety ways. They have the minimum amount of time to waste on details. In addition, the Promoter cannot chat about other people with the Implementor, because the Implementor does not reveal any personal details. The Promoter finds this type of salesperson too boring and does not feel accepted by them.

THE RELATOR

The Relator is a mixture of the Yellow and the Green colour styles.

For the Relator, their private and professional lives are equally important. In both areas, they try to establish positive relationships with those around them, and usually they succeed thanks to their warm-hearted, understanding and easygoing nature. The Relator is good at working in teams and maintaining a pleasant working atmosphere. People are much more important to them than the mere execution of tasks.

What the Relator wants first is to establish a personal relationship between themselves and you as a salesperson. They will feel good about buying from you only if they feel they can trust you. They have a fear of being cheated and so they want to get to know you before they do business with you.

Relators will follow your presentation very attentively. They are good listeners and have very analytical minds that can follow complex solutions. But they do not want to try out new products. They are more interested in hearing who has tried them out and how they were satisfied with them. You should not question the Relator's caution and scepticism. They react sensitively to criticism and tend to take it personally.

The Relator is not the "boss" type. They find it difficult establishing their authority over others. They prefer to make decisions in close consultation with others. You might think them too slow and cautious, but you must also admire their calm and collected air. Above all, do not pressurise them: The Relator does not like stress and prefers to dictate the pace of negotiations themselves. On the other hand, they are very steadfast. They are the type who will prefer to do business with you personally in future, so do not send your colleagues without proper introduction and "due process". They do not like change and need a long time to adapt to it. When they get to know you better, they are very loyal and are not the type to "leave" you to look for more favourable offers elsewhere.

The Relator is most likely to have problems with salespeople of these types:

- *Conductor*: A Red salesperson will probably not take the time to establish a basis of trust, as they do not consider it important. However, the Relator needs this basis of trust, and is unwilling to negotiate without it. The Relator has problems with the Conductor's bossy, dominant manner. They are afraid the Conductor is trying to talk them into buying something they do not need. However, if Relators do not indicate their unwillingness clearly enough, that is exactly what will happen. The Relator will probably withdraw from the deal the very next day and look for a salesperson who has more time for them and to listen to their needs.

The Relator

Goal	To help others, familiarity, harmony, realising ideas, stability
Method	Listens, asks questions, looks for common solutions
Strengths	Tolerant, reliable, loyal, honest; can develop the procedures and techniques necessary to solve a problem
Weaknesses	Finds it difficult to make decisions, often too compliant, unforgiving
Negative impression	Interfering, unobjective, hesitant
Positive impression	Understanding, helpful, sincere
Fears	Conflict, great pressure, loss of relationship

- *Analyser:* The Blue salesperson and the Relator live in two quite different worlds. The Analyser has their sights fixed on the product and the deal, whereas the Relator first wants to know who they are dealing with. As Analysers do not reveal much about themselves, the Relator finds the atmosphere too impersonal. They do not really trust the Analyser and, in the end, they will not buy from them. Besides, they want to be inspired, they have a wealth of ideas, and the Analyser picks holes in them too quickly.
- *Implementor:* Their exact opposite! The Relator cannot understand this Red-Blue salesperson's striving for perfection, as there is no such thing as perfection in inter-human relations. The Relator has ideas and wants to put them forward, but they are far from perfect. With the Implementor, too, the Relator will not find the personal touch they so appreciate, and they become aware that the Implementor disapproves of the fact that they cannot accept "the perfect solutions" the salesperson presents. But before they can enter into a business relationship

with the Implementor, the Relator needs to know who they are doing business with, and the Implementor does not really understand this concept or how to reach over to that zone.

THE SUPPORTER

The Supporter is the Green style through and through. They are

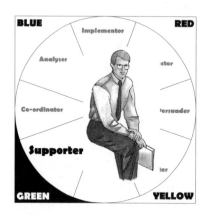

easygoing, likeable and constant, considerate, patient and always ready to help those they consider their friends – what more could you want?

They establish close relationships with a small group of people. If you win Supporters as your customers, the relationships could well continue for many years. The Supporter needs no large audience or theatricals. You will find it difficult to talk properly to them at a trade fair. In their office, on the other hand, they are relaxed and listen attentively to your presentation. They want to buy tried and tested products from you. They appreciate things that do not change much. They need a lot of support and encouragement if they are to be persuaded to buy a new product. They are very knowledgeable in their field, in which they work very efficiently and with great application, and you will have to be well-informed if you want to impress them with your presentation. If you fail to make an impression this time, they may still give you a pat on the back when you leave and express the hope that you can provide them with better information next time.

The Supporter sometimes has difficulties bringing things to a close, or in completing processes, and will then have problems keeping to a schedule. They do not like making decisions and may take a long time to make up their mind to close the deal.

The Supporter

Goal	Stability, familiar surroundings, realising plans
Method	Appropriate, constant
Strengths	Great enthusiasm for special projects/people; is able to develop appropriate techniques for problem-solving
Weaknesses	Passive resistance to change
Negative impression	Conformist, bows to pressure from superiors and colleagues
Positive impression	Always willing to help friends and acquaintances
Fears	Change, disorder

The Supporter is most likely to have problems with salespeople of the following types:

- *Implementor*: The Supporter has difficulties accepting the reserved air of the Blue-Red salesperson, it makes them feel inferior. They are afraid that the Implementor will press them to accept a solution they do not really want. Moreover, they do not trust this salesperson and find them too reticent and cold.

- *Conductor*: The Supporter is not forceful enough to counter the dominance and resoluteness of the Red salesperson and will yield – albeit reluctantly. If they have objections to a product, they will try to wriggle out of the situation by withdrawing into a position of inner resistance and refusing to make a decision. This, in turn, annoys the Conductor, who will try to pressurise them. The Supporter will be glad to see the back of the Conductor and will then set about finding a more understanding salesperson.

- *Persuader*: The Supporter mistrusts the Red-Yellow salesperson's very friendly overtures. They, in turn, are conscious of the Persuader's disapproval because they, the Supporter, do not make up their mind quickly enough to please the salesperson. The Persuader offers them too many innovative products/services and solutions and is constantly trying to persuade them to modernise in order to keep up-to-date with the latest technology. However, offers that so clearly entail change touch on deep-seated fears within the Supporter. They need more time to consider them, more time than the Persuader is willing to allow.

THE CO-ORDINATOR

The Co-ordinator is a combination of Blue and Green. From the

Greens, they take their great sense of loyalty and their willingness to help. The high standards they set themselves show the Blue element in their make-up. As customers, they expect a lot of themselves and of others. They work very carefully and precisely and with great discipline. And they expect you to do the same. If your presentation is chaotic or disorganised, you will irritate a Co-ordinator. They always know exactly what they are doing, they work systematically and with great perseverance. They will discuss the advantages and disadvantages of your product at great length before they make up their mind whether to buy. They will close the deal only if they are absolutely convinced that your product is the right one and that the purchase is necessary. But they do not like making decisions. They like to collect a wealth of facts and details beforehand, so that they can be sure they are not making a mistake. They are conventional, do not like risks or change, and so they tend to prefer conventional products. If they are forced to buy a really new product, they will need even more information beforehand.

If they have objections against your product, they will state them so diplomatically that you might overlook how important these objections are to them. However, you can rest assured that they will be honest and open in their dealings with you. If they learn to respect you, they will be very loyal. They will honour agreements made, and will not question them again the next time you visit. They prefer working with the same group of people as far as possible, and so they would like your business partnership to be a long-term one. Your presentation should be well-structured and you should allow enough time for it. Co-ordinators do not like stress or chaos. Neither do they like being asked personal questions. They will not always say what they are thinking, even less what they feel. It will be a long time before they trust you, because they have a deep-rooted fear of being used. They prefer the company of others who are like them, and so they will expect you to go a long way to suit them.

The Co-ordinator

Goal	To be correct, security, realisation of plans and co-ordination
Method	Collects information and evaluates in depth
Strengths	Is very exact, reliable, good at conceptualisation
Weaknesses	Inflexible, high standards are a hindrance, hesitates
Negative impression	Reserved, suspicious, too objective
Positive impression	Concerned, explains well, is loyal, diplomatic
Fears	Emotions, irrational behaviour

The Co-ordinator is most likely to have problems with salespeople of the following styles:

- *Conductor*: In negotiations with the Red salesperson, a Co-ordinator easily feels pressurised and put under stress. They need a lot of time and information to help them make their decision, both of which the Red salesperson often fails to take into consideration. The Conductor will often offer them innovative products but fail to provide the required support and encouragement that are necessary for a Co-ordinator in this situation.

- *Persuader*: The Red-Yellow salesperson is too "over the top" for the Co-ordinator, who is easily overwhelmed by the strength of the Persuader's willpower and the pressure to close a deal. The Persuader will often recommend a product or a solution because they themselves feel good about it, which is something the Co-ordinator finds hard to accept.
- *Promoter*: The Yellow salesperson is too superficial for the Co-ordinator's taste and just talks too much. The Promoter's often disjointed and chatty presentation is not logical enough for them, and they just cannot take it seriously. They do not want to know *who* has already bought the product. They want to know *why* it is so good. The Co-ordinator reacts with suspicion to the Promoter's conversational tone and over-friendly manner.

THE ANALYSER

The Analyser is a pure Blue style. They are so cautious,

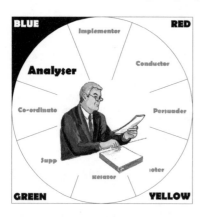

disciplined and conscientious that they will buy only products they feel they can recommend 100%. They have a highly analytical mind and can follow the most complicated presentations easily. In fact, as customers, they are particularly interested in presentations, and expect you to provide as much information and as many details as possible. They also have a keen intuition that often helps them to make the right decision and to avoid mistakes. But they need time for this and will not be hurried.

Analysers will often greet you suspiciously, waiting to see what you have to offer. They will give you no quarter. If something goes wrong with the deal, it will be your fault. They know exactly what they want to ask you, and will work through their list of questions just as they have planned. They prefer a peaceful, non-hectic atmosphere. In negotiations, they sometimes seem a little reserved, as they tend to think longer than other people before answering. This is simply because it is important to them to give the right answer. They hardly ever speak about their feelings. Their family, their closest and most familiar surroundings, are just as important to them as their profession, but they will not tell you about them, nor do they want to hear about your family.

The Analyser

Goal	To be correct, predictable, good reputation, to integrate their plans into an overall concept
Method	Detailed research until they find the right answer
Strengths	Conscientious, analytical thinking, intuitive
Weaknesses	Mistrust, stubbornness, inflexibility
Negative impression	Cool, inaccessible, indifferent
Positive impression	Exact, reliable, astute
Fears	Sudden change, being made a fool of

The Analyser is most likely to have problems with salespeople of the following types:
- *Persuader*: Just as Analysers do not like to express their own feelings, they dislike others doing so. As the Red-Yellow

salesperson is very expressive, however, the two will have great difficulty in making an emotional connection. The Analyser just cannot share the Persuader's basic optimism and, as the solutions the Persuader suggests often mean change, they find it very difficult to accept them.

- *Promoter*: If this Yellow salesperson lets slip just one offhand remark about the Analyser, the latter will find it hard to forget it. The Analyser just does not warm to talkative and enthusiastic people. They will not be swept away by a forceful presentation, but will remain sceptical and cautious. As the Promoter leaves many of their questions unanswered, they consider them incompetent.
- *Relator*: The Green salesperson is far too sensitive for the Analyser. They just prefer to keep their distance, so they cannot share the Relator's desire for a more personal, confidential tone.

THE IMPLEMENTOR

The Implementor is a mixture of Blue and Red. This means the

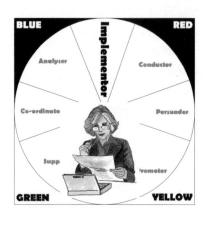

Implementor combines thorough, well-thought out actions with a desire to make their own decisions. Implementors are abstract thinkers, and are very creative and competitive. As a customer, they expect you to provide a clever but well-considered solution in a well-structured, competent presentation. If you have convinced them, they will make up their mind then and there.

However, they try to delay making long-term decisions on very large-scale projects, as they cannot easily foresee the consequences. Their drive for perfection and desire to sound out all possibilities sometimes get in the way when they must make important decisions. On the other hand, they are very quick thinkers, and their ambition spurs their analytical mind on to even greater achievements. They are sometimes overcome by the fact that it is just not possible to foresee all eventualities and take everything into consideration. They can therefore find it difficult to maintain a positive attitude. They will always find something to niggle about, even when you have explained everything right down to the smallest detail.

Implementors have an open mind towards new products and ideas, and they like pioneering, sounding out all the possibilities and solving problems. If they make a mistake, they will be angry – wrongly – with you. Even a long time afterwards, they will not give up trying to find new arguments and facts to prove that their position was correct. They may seem reserved and cold. They can be very authoritarian if you do not take any notice of their requirements and try to fob them off with a superficial presentation.

The Implementor

Goal	Excellence, results, position, finding and realising creative ideas
Method	Sounds out all possibilities, decisions
Strengths	Likes challenge, thoroughness, constancy, can draw up comprehensive concepts and get others to realise them
Weaknesses	Too self-critical, has a tendency to see things in a negative light
Negative impression	Authoritarian, impatient, reserved
Positive impression	Helpful, industrious
Fears	Failure, lack of order

The Implementor is likely to have most problems with salespeople of the following types:

- *Promoter*: The Yellow salesperson is too superficial and hasty for the Implementor's taste. They talk too much without thinking things through first. The Implementor is quick to notice when the Promoter is talking "hot air". As Implementors are not overly interested in their fellow human beings, they certainly do not want to listen to the Promoter's endless stories about other people.

- *Relator*: The Implementor often knows – subconsciously, at least – that the Green-Yellow salesperson would like to hear some personal details about their personal or professional lives, but even still they are unwilling to reveal themselves and their feelings. Moreover, they do not like people giving them clever advice. They want information and facts, and then they prefer to decide on their own whether they need the product the Relator is offering.

- *Supporter*: The Green salesperson is too moderate and too ready to conform for the Implementor, who needs greater challenges and prefers to discuss the pros and cons of a product. But if they raise objections, the Supporter politely dodges the issue and does not say what they think. The Implementor cannot understand the Supporter's continuing friendliness, as they are much quicker to frustration and anger if the negotiations do not go as they expect them to.

CONCLUSION

I am sure you have already identified several of your customers as one of the eight types: Conductor, Persuader, Promoter, Relator, Supporter, Co-ordinator, Analyser or Implementor. This "insight" into human behaviour should make it easier for you to understand why you get on well with some customers and not so well with others, why you sell quite easily to some customers and almost never to others, why relationships are sustained with some customers and break down far too quickly with others, and why it is that the majority of your sales over time will be with people similar to yourself. Consider the implications of this in terms of industry analysis, territory management and key account management.

Chris Jones is a business development executive for an engineering firm. He sells a range of iron products to dealers all over the country. Chris completed four computerised competency analyses as part of a sales development process in his company. One of these tests revealed that he was a Supporter.

We looked at his top 50 customers who generated 83% of his business and found that 39 of them were Green. Chris knows each one intimately and is very happy with this analysis. Two of his customers were Red, three Yellow and six Blue.

When we analysed 50 prospects that he had been unable to sell to over the previous two years, we found a revealing contrast – 40 of them, at least, were his opposite colour. He now admits he had given up on them for all the wrong reasons and set a plan to sell them "as they were" and not "as he was". Within six months, he had increased his overall business by 37% with this group alone.

Top salespeople learn from these kinds of insight. They recognise very quickly what their customer expects of them and they can adapt to these expectations. The best salespeople are often very similar in their basic style. In the next chapter, we will look at what distinguishes the top salesperson.

7:

HOW TO BECOME A TOP SALESPERSON

You want to be a top salesperson? Then just look and see how other salespeople made it to the top. Three things distinguish them:
- Ambition, commitment and persistence
- Flexibility
- Finding the appropriate sector.

You do not have to "learn" commitment and ambition. They are probably a matter of course for you. However, there are some things about the other two factors that you are perhaps not aware of.

WHAT DISTINGUISHES THE TOP SALESPERSON?

In its December 1998 issue, the German magazine *acquisa* published a study on the top 500 salespeople. Together with the *Scheelen-Institut für Managementberatung und Bildungsmarketing* and using the SUCCESS INSIGHTS method, this study analysed the decisive factors that made these people top salespeople. Above all, the salespeople were asked about their basic motives and their typical attitudes to customers; their answers were analysed by computer.

Green-Yellow: An ideal combination for sales

The results of the *acquisa* analysis showed that most top salespeople belonged to four particular styles: They are Promoters, Relators, Persuaders or Supporters.

Remember the characteristics of the main styles: Promoters and Persuaders are Yellow types, Relators and Supporters Green types. What all four have in common is that they like contact with other people and get on well with them. The Yellow type is more enthusiastic, the Green somewhat more restrained and more constant. As *acquisa* put it: "They all have a high degree of social competence and the ability to establish profitable relationships with others".

They are extremely sensitive, open to their customers and have the gift of being able to adapt to their customers. They ask questions and take the time to find out what the customer's specific requirements are. They have a natural interest in getting to know and understanding others. This predestines them for a career where they are constantly establishing contact with other people and adapting to them. All four styles tend to act on the level of relationships. They are less interested in facts and things. They have an instinct for the needs of others and act more "from the heart than from the head".

The advantages of the four Yellow-Green types are:

- They are good at establishing contact and are enthusiastic
- They have a feeling for and are sensitive to the customer's requirements
- They establish lasting bonds with customers
- They are good at follow-up and customer service.

The Blue-Yellow cross-type: The ideal salesperson

In our experience as sales trainers, there is another SUCCESS INSIGHTS style who makes a very successful salesperson: the Blue-Yellow cross-type.

This style combines the qualities of the Promoter with those of the Analyser. The Promoter in them gives them the necessary *élan*, allowing them to convey enthusiasm to their customers, break the ice, establish a relationship and present their product or service in lively terms. The Blue elements in their make-up ensure that they do not get "carried away". They prevent a salesperson of this style talking their customer's ears off endlessly and aimlessly, ensuring instead that they have drawn up a structured plan of action and do not forget while talking that they should be working towards closing the deal. Blue-Yellow salespeople are also experts in their field, who know all about their product and are always right up-to-date. The Yellow aspects of their character, on the other hand, prevent the Analyser getting bogged down in research and data-gathering and make sure that they "go public" and present their facts to the customer.

In other words, the Blue-Yellow cross-type:
- Has product competence, detailed knowledge
- Is calm and good at organising their time
- Does structured preparation

and, on the other hand:
- Is enthusiastic, enjoys selling
- Likes contact with people and is good at establishing relationships
- Is creative in problem-solving.

WHICH SALESPERSON IS BEST SUITED TO WHICH SECTOR/FIELD?

The top salespeople described above will probably cut a good figure whatever sector they go to work in. And yet salespeople require different talents from sector to sector. In its study, *acquisa* took a closer look at the specific differences between seven industries, establishing which methods are most advantageous in which sector. The results of this study will give you some idea of where you would be most successful.

Pharmaceutical representative

Implementors are particularly well represented among the top salespeople in the pharmaceutical sector. The combination styles of the Analyser/Co-ordinator and the Persuader are also successful.

In order to sell in the pharmaceutical sector, you have to be conscientious, precise and good at finding special solutions. Salespeople here have to have a high degree of specialist knowledge. Implementors can also make use of their talent for analytical thinking. As they have a great capacity for understanding, they can appreciate their customers' complex problems. They do not allow the job to put them under pressure. On the contrary, they experience it as a challenge in the positive sense. They are very result-oriented and able to present material they consider important in an impressive way. At the same time, they are able to assert themselves and successfully conduct the tough price negotiations that are customary in this sector. They bear in mind not only their own financial interests but also the customer's requirements. They are able to maintain long-lasting customer relations, a very important factor in this sector where new customers do not "grow" overnight.

But this is exactly where their weak points lie: They are not good at winning new customers. Also, they like to potter around by themselves and develop solutions on their own, without others being involved in or having access to their plans.

The combination style Analyser/Co-ordinator is also successful in this sector, because they have a similar talent for analysing complex systems and adapting to the customer. However, they lack assertiveness and are not communicative enough, whereas Persuaders have a great deal of *élan* and the will to achieve good results, although they may not always offer a result that has been carefully thought through.

Key account manager

You cannot lump all the successful salespeople who are responsible for key accounts together. The top people have different behaviour profiles. The most widely represented group is that of the Promoter, followed by the Persuader and the Relator. Of course, there are also some successful Supporters and Co-ordinators in this sector, and a few Analysers. The only group not represented is Conductors, which can be said to be valid for the whole profession: The typical key account manager is not a Conductor.

However, it is not the pure or extreme styles who feature among the most successful key account managers, but combination styles. A key account manager is often distinguished by a mixture of a capacity for enthusiasm and openness paired with respectability.

In order to go far in this sector, you need a good proportion of characteristics from each colour type. It makes sense that this should be so, because looking after large-scale customers demands flexibility and a pronounced talent for adapting to various characters and their requirements. The combination types are also good at handling groups, especially if they have strong Yellow aspects: They like an audience. They are able to think strategically, which is important when negotiating with large-scale customers. And their follow-up is persistent. They have to be able to assert themselves against the pressure that large-scale customers can exert. At the same time, they must not lose sight of their company's interests.

It is hardly surprising that there are so many Promoters in this sector. The Promoter's obliging nature and sociability make it easy for them to deal with many different customers. If they also have Green aspects, they are even more suited to looking after customers long-term, as they then ask more questions and go into things in more depth. If they tend towards the Red, they find it easier to assert themselves and to convince others of what they have to offer.

The fact that so many different behavioural types are successful in this area reflects the fact that a key account manager's customers will vary according to the product they have to offer. If the key account manager works in an enterprise connected with technology, their Blue element will certainly be stronger, because they will have to answer so many detailed questions, whereas in a service business the Yellow aspects of strength in relationships and social competence become more important.

Car salespeople

The Promoter and Persuader styles are predominant among top car salespeople. The Relators are rarer. So successful salespeople in this sector are not the mechanical freaks and cool-headed engineers you might expect.

When buying a car, other factors are more important than the mere question of superior technology. People buy cars because they want particular extras or because they covet the image and the social standing they associate with a particular make or model. Successful car salespeople must convince their customers on an emotional level and be able to activate their feelings in favour of a particular car.

The best in the sector also have their own financial interest in mind. They can get enthusiastic about the aesthetically pleasing lines of a new model, but they still keep a cool head. They do their sums and work out exactly which customers it is worth their while to cultivate. This is where, above all, the Persuaders come into their own. Their Red aspects give them the necessary egoistic streak. All outstanding car salespeople also have strong Yellow elements. They do not wait until customers come to them, but will go out looking for new customers wherever they can. Their follow-up, however, is weaker, because by then they have lost most of their interest in their customer. If the Green elements in their make-up are stronger, they will look after their regular customers better.

Top car salespeople are motivated by lucrative remuneration systems that reward their commitment with cash bonuses.

Service providers

The majority of the top salespeople in the service sector are Green-Yellow: Promoters, Relators and Supporters dominate the field here. Their great strength lies in the field of human relationships, and they are active almost exclusively on this level. They are sensitive and understanding and can comprehend the customer's requirements. They will phone customers on their own initiative to offer them something new. They are the ideal relationship managers. Their "Green" attributes mean that they are also able to analyse complex problems and work systematically towards a solution. In contrast to the pure Yellow types, they keep their promises.

Their weakness lies in the consistent closing of the deal. They find it difficult to draw clear lines and demand that the customer choose whether they want to do business or not. For them as salespeople, there is more to it than just financial gain. Social factors are often more important, which shows a certain selflessness: They would rather do without the deal now and hope for better luck next time than risk ruining their good relationship with the customer.

Salespeople for products requiring intensive consultation

Selling such products requires a salesperson who is patient, can understand how others feel and who can convince others. No wonder, then, that the top people in this sector are Promoters, Persuaders and Relators. They have the power to convince the customer how useful their new product is. They can put themselves in their customers' position and offer solutions tailor-made to suit their problems. This means asking questions, being able to listen to and to analyse the answers and also being able to persuade the customer of the advantages of new, complex solutions. The top salespeople often have the gifts of the Analyser: They can pick up the essential details of meetings, follow questions through and analyse problems precisely. In addition, they can also develop new product or service solutions.

Insurance salespeople

In this sector, too, the outstanding figures are Relators and Persuaders. They are extremely persuasive and eloquent, but also sensitive enough to appreciate their customer's requirements and to adapt to suit them. They are relationship-oriented and are motivated by their own achievements when they see that they have built up a good relationship with a customer. And so they will invest a great deal of time and energy in establishing such relationships.

On the other hand, specialist knowledge is also very important in this sector. Insurance salesperson must have a great deal of specialist knowledge on a wide range of products at their fingertips when advising their customers.

If they are Persuaders, they are particularly successful in canvassing new customers. It is no problem for them to address potential new customers, on the street if necessary. Their weakness is their tendency to talk too much (about themselves) and lose sight of the customer.

Salespeople in Direct Marketing

Financial motives are just as important to the top salespeople in direct marketing as the desire for self-realisation. They are ambitious, determined, and eager to get to the top and enjoy competition. Here, for once, Conductors or other salespeople with strong Red characteristics are more common. It follows that success and status are important for these styles. Closing the deal is their great strength. They want to see a signed contract on the table in front of them. However, they may lack sensitivity and empathy. They like fresh challenges and are ideally suited to tackling seemingly hopeless projects.

CONCLUSION

The *acquisa* study showed that most successful salespeople belong to the Green-Yellow group. Depending on the sector in which they work and the product they sell, the mix will be more or less colourful, with the addition of Blue, or more rarely Red, characteristics. Red-Green cross-types are hardly ever found in sales.

If you happen to be a Red-Green cross-type, this does not mean that you should change jobs. But it does mean that it is more of a conscious effort for you to adapt to your customers than it is for other colour styles whose natural behaviour is more akin to that of the top salespeople described here.

The results of the *acquisa* study clearly mirror the current trend in sales towards customer-orientation and skilful relationship management. If you want to achieve top performance in sales, you should develop these sides of your character.

You can change by realising who you are and what is your natural style and then modifying your behaviour.

In this section, you have analysed your selling style. And now you know what abilities top salesperson possess and to which colour types most of them belong.

PART 2:

SELLING COMPETENTLY AND CONVINCINGLY

8:

How to Recognise Your Customer's Style

In order to adapt your communication and selling style to best suit your customer, you must be able to define what style they are. You have learned how to do this already. The advantage is that you know what to expect and are always in a more advanced state of "readiness" than your customer. You behave in the way you know promises most success with this customer. Remember: One tiny step is enough. Many races are won by no more than a nose!

When you analyse your customers and define their colour style, you should always remember two things:

- Observe carefully. There is no hurry to decide a customer's colour category. Remember that almost everyone will display elements of two, if not three colour styles.
- Do not be surprised if your customer behaves in a completely unexpected way now and again. It could be that they are under stress or displaying their natural style.

The key to communication is to observe and respect differences. After a meeting with a customer, train yourself by writing down all the behavioural characteristics you noticed in them. Next time you meet this customer, check whether you can spot similar characteristics or notice new ones.

Watch for these four general areas:

- The volume and form of words

- Their tone of voice
- The rate at which they speak (words per minute)
- Their body language.

Pay attention to the small details which are often revealing: Handshake, pictures on a desk, eye contact, hand movements, calm or hectic gestures, etc ...

Practise your skills by paying attention to such details when talking to customers and colleagues – but not at the expense of the conversation and perhaps someone's friendship. People do not like being watched, and your aim is not to become a private detective but an attentive, sensitive person to maximise the potential of the communication.

CHECKLIST FOR CUSTOMER BEHAVIOUR

Remember your last meeting with a specific customer and write down what you noticed about the following points:

1. How was the customer's handshake?
2. What did you notice on their desk?
3. Who kicked off the conversation?
4. How would you describe the customer's tone of voice?
5. In which situations did the tone of their voice change?
6. What did their body language tell you about them during your meeting?
7. Was their attention occasionally diverted? If so, by what?
8. Did they ask a lot of questions? Were the questions they asked productive in terms of the purpose of your meeting?
9. When expressing their opinion, did they use expressions like "I think ...", "In my opinion ..." or did they choose expressions like "You would think that ..." or "One would expect ..."?
10. Did the customer look you in the eye or avoid eye contact?

Below is a description of the behavioural characteristics of the four customer styles. Of course, not every Red customer will display all characteristics of the Red customer described here. But if you do meet a customer who is "Red" or has strong "Red" elements in their make-up, you will be able to identify them easily with the help of this description.

THE RED CUSTOMER

Surroundings and atmosphere

Their desk reflects their importance: They bear as much

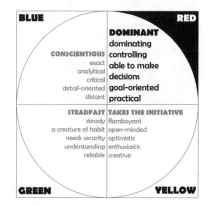

responsibility on their shoulders as there is material on their desk. You can see that their work is well-organised. The different projects and documents are all in neat piles. The message to the visitor is clear: "I've got a lot of work to do and no time to waste".

There are certificates awarded to the company on the walls and awards for merit in their work. Or certificates showing their commitment in work-related areas, in their position as the president of a professional association or as an honorary member of an institute. There are also large calendars on the walls with entries for their many appointments and business trips.

The furnishings of their office radiate power and success. The desk and the other furniture are large and dominate the room. They also create distance. It is not unusual for a Red customer to ask you to take a seat on the other side of their desk so that this huge piece of furniture acts as a barrier between the two of you while you speak. Or they will offer you a seat in a formal seating group that is not built for comfort but to impress and dominate. Being closed and formal, the seating arrangement does not promote contact but reflects the balance of power.

Typical behaviour

The Red customer tends to greet you in a cool, businesslike manner with a firm handshake. They will scrutinise you without any particular sign of warmth. If you are male, you will find yourself wondering whether your tie is straight; if you are female, whether your mascara is smudged.

The Red customer's voice is strong and powerful. Their choice of words reflect their self-confidence and they tell you what they want without further ado. They often emphasise the meaning of their words by means of linear hand movements. Their whole bearing expresses self-confidence and a trace of superiority.

Their basic attitude is: "Let's throw this sales professional off balance". They believe that they will get the best deal only if they can break you down, psychologically and commercially. In their opinion, you always have to fight hard to get a low price and the best conditions: "No salesperson would do their customer a favour voluntarily".

And so they will treat you in a very authoritarian manner from the start. They do not necessarily mean to be unfriendly, but the message is clear: "I'll know when you are trying to cheat me, don't think I won't". Sometimes this makes them appear somewhat defiant, as if they were saying to you "Just don't try selling me anything! I've already got everything I need!".

They will take the reins firmly in their hand from the start and tell you in no uncertain terms what they want and what they do not want. Their wishes are dictated by their own ego and by their desire for clear structures. Their attitude towards you is uncooperative and cold. In their presence, you feel a strong pressure that feels as if it could crush and paralyse you in the first few moments. Reading between the lines, the message is "I know what I need, so don't waste my time trying to change my mind".

Delivering your presentation could be difficult. The Red customer will interrupt or contradict you frequently. The reason they do this is their deep-rooted need to be constantly reaffirming that they are the number one: "I'll show you who is in control here". They appear argumentative, and will put forward one objection after another. Every time you answer one of their objections, they will find something else they are doubtful about: "You can't win, you know. And here's another reason why not". They lay traps for you and, like so many before you, you will probably walk straight into them. They want you to start defending yourself and your product. Once they have got you on the defensive, they have as good as won.

And if they do not manage to defeat you, they probably will not buy, unless they really need your product desperately. Once they have got you on the defensive (and by now you will be pretty unnerved), they will try to dictate the terms, and the terms they suggest will seem completely unacceptable to you.

From the beginning of the negotiations, you will have a strong desire to give way (if you are a Yellow/Green), to stage a showdown (if you are a Red/Blue) or to withdraw (as a Blue/Green). Being totally aware of your own natural behaviour – your own colour style – will help you to understand how the Red's behaviour will affect you in a certain way. Your reaction and responses are therefore within your own control – unlike your customer's unaware and spontaneous approach. Appreciating their style for what it is ("it's NOT a personal attack") gives you a huge psychological advantage in the sales process.

Typical behavioural patterns for a Red customer
- Appears determined and dominant but not unfriendly

- Chooses the topics and takes control of the conversation
- Seems cool, independent and aggressive
- Proceeds quickly and impatiently
- Looks you challengingly in the eye
- Wants quick results, makes concrete demands
- Questions things, contradicts, gives you little credit
- Displays low tolerance of the feelings, attitudes and suggestions of others.

Typical communication style

The Red customer asks a lot of "What?" questions:

- What solution does your product offer for my problems?
- What extras/discount can you offer?
- What is the price?
- What do my competitors use?

They speak quickly and often interrupt you. The only subjects that can capture their attention for any period of time are all related to profit, competition and advantages. Everything they say is geared to getting results. They use words like "today", "now", "immediately", "the best", "the first", "optimum".

Typical questions from a Red customer

- How much does it cost?
- Can I adapt it?
- When can you deliver?
- Will I be the first in the area with one?
- How many horse-power does it have?
- What's its capacity?
- Is this the biggest and best model available?
- How long is the warranty period?
- Is it new?
- Why was it designed like that? It would be much better if ...
- What sort of company is it you represent?

The Red customer's expectations

Above all, the Red customer expects you to be competent. They do not want your visit to be a waste of their time. They want you to present your product quickly and clearly. Moreover, they are not interested in the conventional, but expect you to show them your latest and most innovative products.

How will you recognise a Conductor?

- They are well-prepared and focus their full attention on the meeting
- For them, only results count
- They keep their eye on the time, and the meeting proceeds very efficiently
- They show no particular consideration for your interests as a salesperson or for you personally
- They react with annoyance and impatience if your presentation or the meeting drag on.

How will you recognise a Persuader?

- Results count, but they can also see your side of things as a salesperson
- They refer to "their team" in the course of the meeting
- They show their enthusiasm for your product
- They give you credit for a good presentation
- They prefer products that are forward-looking and represent a challenge.

THE YELLOW CUSTOMER

Surroundings and atmosphere

Their desk is untidy – covered in mountains of papers and documents. The most fascinating

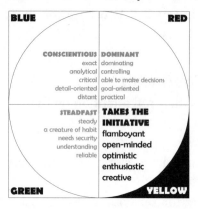

thing is that, in spite of the chaos, the Yellow customer knows where everything is and in which pile they can find which document. Nevertheless, at least once while you are with them, they will have to search for something that they cannot put their hand on straight away. While they are hunting, they will tell you the latest joke, so you will pass the time pleasantly until they have found whatever they are looking for.

On the walls of the Yellow customer's office, you will find bits of paper with personally motivating slogans and notes. They also find motivation in posters showing adventurous scenes, for example a climber hanging over an abyss or an attitude poster like "Attitude is everything".

The furniture in their office is arranged in open formations, and is airy and friendly. This is one customer who definitely will not offer you a seat on the other side of their desk, but will sit down with you in a comfortable seating group arranged in such a way that it creates an atmosphere that is informal and encourages contact. The Yellow customer will interrupt your negotiations once or twice to answer the phone and, when they return to you, they will sit down on a different chair each time. This is an expression of their dynamism and need for change. They will certainly offer you something to drink, if they have not chosen to meet you in a restaurant in the first place.

Typical behaviour

The thing that strikes you most about the Yellow customer is that they do most of the talking, even though it is you who are supposed to be presenting your product to them. But, for the Yellow customer, it is not the product that is of prime importance. The first thing they want to know is *who* they will be buying it from. And they also want you to know who you are selling to. And so you will first talk about general and personal details. They will ask you about your company or about mutual acquaintances. And they will tell you a lot about who they are and their company. Their basic attitude is: "I like talking to people, even if I don't want to buy anything – I might make a new friend!".

The Yellow customer is always friendly and obliging, even when discussing controversial subjects. Their smile is open, they are very obliging and they underscore their open stance with expressive gestures. They may touch your arm now and again or pat your shoulder to bridge the gap between you. They seem very sure of themselves. You will get the message: "Just look what a nice fellow I am. You've got to like me!".

They laugh a lot, like having fun and acting the clown. They tell jokes or make ironic comments to break up serious negotiations. They will tell you a lot about other people they know. Perhaps they will show you around their company or department, as they assume that you share their love of contact and of meeting new people.

If you are in a restaurant or a room with a view of other people, they will always have one eye on what is going on. This is not an expression of discourtesy towards you but of their inborn curiosity.

They are enthusiastic and encouraging about your presentation, and appear keen and impressed by your product. The message you are getting is: "Hey, aren't we two getting on wonderfully?". They raise no objections (or at least, very few): "I don't believe in making life hard for people". Perhaps they are so enthusiastic about you and your product that they will agree to buy long before you have given them all the information. If they buy, they do so with great *élan*. If not, however, they will not look you in the face and tell you straight out that they are not convinced of your product or that they think it is too expensive. They will not explain why they cannot buy now: "I'm sorry, but I don't think I'm quite ready yet" but are more likely to change the subject and talk about all sorts of other things until you realise that, for today at least, you are getting nowhere.

Typical behavioural patterns for a Yellow customer

- Acts spontaneously and makes decisions from gut feeling
- Is full of enthusiasm, sometimes seems exaggerated and dramatic, talks a lot
- Is easy-going, very friendly and obliging, participates emotionally
- Displays interest and enthusiasm, even if they do not plan to buy
- Their faces always display enthusiasm. If they are not really interested, they will simply stare into space
- Proceeds quickly, jumping from one subject to another
- Forgets time easily
- Has a very optimistic attitude.

Typical communication style

Their questions revolve around the word "Who?":
- Who uses your products?
- Who do you know?
- Who among your acquaintances could extend my network of contacts?

They talk mostly about other people, less about things and abstract concepts. They like to exaggerate and have a great tendency to generalise.

Most of all, they like to talk about "me". Their choice of words is lively and graphic, and they underscore what they say with many gestures and lively facial expressions. Actually, they are acting most of the time, trying out new roles. Their frequent changes of subject will often catch you unawares. You have hardly answered one question when they suddenly move on to the next. This is because they are not really listening to you very attentively.

Typical questions from a Yellow customer
- What will my neighbours/friends say/think?
- Have you had a cup of coffee? Let's have one and talk the matter over
- I would like to buy from you, and you would like to sell to me, but who is going to bear the delivery costs?
- Who's your bet for the championship?
- Can you use photos of my company in your advertising for this product?
- If I use your product and follow your recommendations, will I win something in your competition?
- Does that come in a colour that matches my office?
- If I buy this product, do I get a free trip?
- Who are you? What did you do before this job?
- The competition is a great idea. I'll certainly take part. How about a coffee?

The Yellow Customer's expectations
The Yellow customer expects you to satisfy their curiosity. They are not so much curious about your product, but for news about other people, new jokes, inside information or your own background. They want you to be just as open as they are and to chat with them. They want to get to know you and are

disappointed if you are reticent and refuse to reveal something about yourself. They are also interested in finding out who you know and whether you can pave their way to any new contacts. Your specialist competence is less important.

On the whole, they expect you to take time to talk to them, and will not appreciate your rushing off to the next customer as soon as they have signed the contract.

You should not let their frequent changes of direction while you are talking bother you, and you should not harp on a subject that they consider over and done with. One of their greatest expectations is that you should bring fresh life, something new to their office and not be boring. In addition, they want to learn about your very latest products, so that they can tell others about the latest development on the market.

How will you recognise a Promoter?

- They are more interested in ideas than concrete solutions
- They talk a lot and jump from one topic to another
- They are fascinated by all things new, especially innovative developments
- They are very flexible and can adapt quickly to new situations and people
- They do not want all the details, lengthy presentations or too many facts
- They would prefer to know who is already using the product rather than how the product works.

How will you recognise the Relator?

- They are enthusiastic about new solutions, but do not always think about how they could apply them
- Human relationships are important to them, but they should not be too superficial
- They are very co-operative, very friendly and open during meetings

- Their reaction can be dramatic if you do not pay attention to their requirements
- They do not like confrontation, but strive for harmony and agreement. They will not raise objections openly.

THE GREEN CUSTOMER

Surroundings and atmosphere

The first things you will notice on a Green customer's desk are

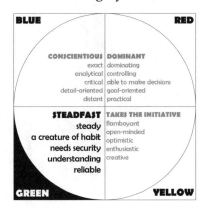

family photos and other personal objects. On the walls, there are also family photos or photos of their colleagues on the last company outing. You will also find personal slogans that motivate them and strengthen their self-confidence.

Their office furnishings are chosen to create a friendly, calming atmosphere. The seating is arranged in open form, informal and encouraging contact. The Green type will also not put a desk between you and them and is more likely to invite you to visit their home.

Typical behaviour

The Green customer is accommodating, friendly and relaxed. They make you feel at home and accepted. However, they still seem thoughtful and cautious. Their basic attitude is: "I don't really want this. The less you say to a salesperson, the less chance there is of you making a bad bargain". That is why, if they do not know you or do not know you well, they will answer in monotones, off-handedly and reservedly. You can almost read their mind: "Do nothing to encourage this salesperson. They'll only talk me into buying something I don't need". Once you get to know them, and if past business deals have been mutually beneficial, they will open up, and their caution will no longer be directed towards you but towards your product. They know that they will not be able to say "No" if you ask directly, and so they try to avoid the situation in the first place.

So they will follow your presentation silently, politely and reservedly. Their attitude is: "Don't think I agree with you just because I'm nodding now and again". They ask a lot of questions and need a lot of information from you. However, they will not bring forward their arguments against your product directly, but will tend to express their doubts in the form of questions. If they want to put off making a decision, they will make excuses and will not tell you openly what is going on. If they are in any doubt, they will not agree to buy the product  immediately, even if they personally like it very much. They like to sleep on their decisions. Or perhaps they want to talk it over with their boss or colleagues. They may order something to keep you happy, just for the sake of peace and quiet – you may have pressurised them too much. However, they will withdraw from the deal later. And even if they do buy in the end, they never seem completely convinced or enthusiastic about their purchase. Their attitude seems to be: "I'm not sure if I'm doing the right thing here".

If they are in a managerial position, they may be even more cautious. They may be even less prepared to try something new and to assume the responsibility for the decision.

Typical behavioural patterns for a Green customer
- Their need to trust you as a salesperson is existential
- They act and make decisions hesitantly

- They do not like conflict, and avoid controversial subjects
- They listen actively to your presentation
- They accept others, and are respectful and friendly
- They look at you in a friendly way if they feel positive but avoid eye contact if there are problems
- They refer to colleagues to hear their opinions
- They are cautious but informal, preferring to be on first-name terms
- They ask a lot of questions
- They express their personal feelings.

Typical communication style

The Green customer concentrates on "Why?":
- Why should I believe what you are telling me?
- Why is your product the best solution?
- Why are you offering me such a generous discount?

The Green customer speaks warmly and calmly and hardly ever raises their voice. They like lengthy discussions – not only about the product itself, but also touching on the advantages the product would bring for them, their family or their team.

Typical questions from a Green customer

- I'll buy what you recommend. How much will it cost me?
- I'm not really interested in what's new on the market this year. I want my old familiar product. How much is it this year?
- Can you still deliver the original product?
- What does everyone else use?
- It's not really a problem, but why is it more expensive today?
- Why have you changed your product? I've only just got used to the old one.
- This is an established, tried and tested product, isn't it?
- There's no hurry, is there?
- What do most other people buy?
- If I order from you, can you deliver within six months?

- Is this device completely safe for my family?
- Can I think it over and get back to you?
- Would you call me back in one week? I would like to have a look at some other offers.

The Green customer's expectations

Above all, the Green customer expects you to be honest and not cheat them. Unfortunately, they will never be quite convinced of this. They expect you to listen attentively and to take note of their requirements. They will invest quite a lot of effort in establishing a deeper relationship with you, and they expect you to make the same effort. You should also be sure to plan enough time for your meetings with Green customers.

They expect you to offer them tried and tested products. You will only be able to interest them in new products when others have tested them first. If you visit this customer frequently, they will expect everything to have remained more or less the same as it was on your last visit, so that you can pick up your relationship exactly where you left off last time. They will also expect you to remember everything they told you in previous meetings.

How will you recognise the Supporter?

- They like making plans and taking plenty of time putting them into action. They have a deep-seated need for clear structures and presentation
- It is very important to them to enter into a deeper personal relationship with you
- They prefer to work with salespeople who support them, share their views and do not question them
- They like established products.

How will you recognise the Co-ordinator?

- With your involvement, they will work out in great detail exactly what their requirements are and what sort of solution they envisage

- They are more intent on the task than on you. It is clear that they prefer to occupy themselves with structures, systems and procedures
- They like to work with realistic deadlines and expects you to honour all deadlines and agreements
- They do not like tasks that are too abstract or salespeople who are too dominant
- They are very constant and loyal.

THE BLUE CUSTOMER

Surroundings and atmosphere

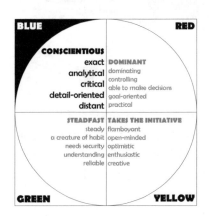

When you arrive in a Blue customer's office, they will already have all the documents relating to your visit in front of them on their desk. The desk itself will be tidy, the shelves and cupboards demonstrating structure and order. On the walls, there will be statistical tables, curves, charts or pictures connected with their work.

Although the furnishings will be friendly and discreet, the seating group will show a desire to prevent closer contact and to maintain a formal atmosphere. You may have to take a seat across the desk from the Blue customer.

Typical behaviour of a Blue customer

The Blue customer greets you in a friendly manner, but is very distant and gets straight down to business. As a person, you interest them only in connection with the business in hand: They will ask you about your qualifications and your company, but they will ask no personal questions. They will also talk very little about themselves and will block questions immediately if you ask them anything personal. All they want is someone who is qualified and competent to sell them a perfect product. Their unvoiced questions are: "Are the salesperson and the product logical, accurate, worth their money, of high-quality and reliable?".

They will have thought beforehand about what they want to achieve in the meeting and may even have made a list. If they have, they will now go through it point-by-point. They are keen to remain firmly in control of the situation so that they can proceed systematically. You will feel as if you were at school again, because  they will remind you of a teacher testing you orally. They will make notes of your answers. They will also have their notes from earlier meetings in front of them and will come back to points that they made a note of then. Their message is clear: "I remember everything and I will notice any contradictions in what you say. You can't pull the wool over my eyes".

They proceed slowly and carefully and will watch you closely. They study your body language to see whether you are telling the truth. Their own body language, however, is very subdued because they do not want to reveal what they are thinking or whether they are going to buy. The Blue customer will keep their distance. If you were to give them a friendly pat on the shoulder at some point in the meeting, they would take it as an attack on their person. They may even go as far as to sit far away from you to prevent this happening.

Their basic attitude to salespeople is: "Study all the written material first, without letting the salespeople hurry you into making a decision". They are deeply suspicious, but this is not personal. They simply want to avoid making a mistake. However, they do not really trust information gained in conversation. They put more faith in what they have read somewhere than in what you tell them. It is also obvious that they would prefer written information rather than listening to you talking at them.

While they listen to your presentation, they seem thoughtful and indifferent. In fact, they are listening very carefully to what you say. But their message is clear: "I need more time to think it over. I need more information ...". Often their questions start with "Show me ...", which states clearly that they have no confidence in words alone. They have a fixation about gathering data and will definitely drive you to the point where you are at a loss for an answer to their questions – unless you are also a Blue.

The Blue customer will only raise objections if they consider you competent enough to answer them. If you try to hurry them into making a decision, they will dodge the issue. They will delay closing the deal or postpone making a decision until another date. They have to think about all this in peace and quiet and read through the documentation thoroughly. They will almost certainly solicit offers from your rivals.

If they are a boss, they will react even more slowly and cautiously, because they have to think even more carefully about every decision when they bear the full responsibility for the outcome.

Typical behavioural patterns for a Blue customer

- Seems serious and reserved
- Is very persistent and asks a lot of questions
- Pace is measured and cautious
- Asks about written material and takes notes
- Organises their time in a very disciplined manner
- Avoids prolonged eye contact
- Likes tight organisation, structure and order.

Typical communication style

Typical questions from a Blue customer begin with "How?":

- How does this product work?
- How do you explain this or that?
- How often has the product been tested already?

They ask concrete questions about concrete details.

Blues speak slowly and carefully, as though they were thinking carefully about each word before it passes their lips. They phrase everything very precisely and their voices hardly alter. They believe that gestures or facial expressions might reveal their thoughts, so they suppress them as far as possible. They can, however, be very diplomatic and often deliver very well-turned and polished phrases.

Typical questions from a Blue customer

- Is this a tried and tested product?
- What else can you tell me about the product?
- What happens if it won't work?
- Are you sure that the product can do all you say it can?
- Is this the best product on the market?
- How much would an extended period of warranty and a maintenance contract cost me?
- Will you be able to keep exactly to my specifications?
- This is not a new method, is it?
- I don't have to make up my mind now, do I?
- Is this a high-quality product?
- How long is the warranty period?
- I need the product in the same colour as the old one. Can you guarantee that?
- Who manufactures your product? Is the manufacturer experienced in this field of production?
- What is your professional background?
- I'm not quite sure whether I have understood you there. Could you explain it again in more detail?

The Blue customer's expectations

They really would like you to be a competent salesperson and able to offer them a first-class product. But they are already expecting to be disappointed. And so they will settle for your explaining everything as well and in as much detail as you can and then leaving plenty of written material for them to study. Then they expect you to leave them plenty of time to make up their mind and not to hurry them. Above all, they do not want you to get on their nerves, bore them with your talk or ask them about their private life.

They expect you to provide a constant and professional service with a minimum of fuss and maximum security.

How will you recognise the Analyser?

- They like working in step-by-step processes with agendas and minutes
- They prefer written information with lots of details
- They are very precise and need a lot of time to gather data
- They do not enjoy making decisions
- They do not like change, new products, unexpected visitors or any other surprises.

How will you recognise the Implementor?

- They like deliberating over things and coming up with new solutions. They are quite open to new products as long as they receive a lot of information beforehand and enough time to think about it
- They have a very businesslike manner, and are punctual, very precise and formal
- They do not like digressions from the subject in hand, interruptions, chaotic presentations or personal anecdotes
- They like to get their own way, enjoys challenge and has a strong will. They see tough negotiations as a challenge in the positive sense

- They need time and do not like others trying to dictate the pace.

EXERCISE:
CUSTOMER RELATIONSHIP ANALYSIS

Would you like to test your knowledge on one of your customers? If so, carry out the customer relationship analysis shown below.

Think of one of your customers and mark with a cross in each of the four columns the characteristics that apply to them. The concentration of the crosses you make will give you some idea of which combination type your customer is.

Compare your results with the SUCCESS INSIGHTS wheel. Which one of the eight main styles would you say your customer is?

EXERCISE:
CUSTOMER RELATIONSHIP ANALYSIS

What colour is my customer?

Customer name: _____

Company: _____

Personality	Dominant	Influencing	Steady	Conscientious
Reactions	Quick answers	Speaks freely	Slow/hesitant	Unfathomable
Clothing	Professional	Fashionable	Conventional	Conservative
Car	Impressive	Sporty	Functional	Traditional
Eye contact	Direct	Warm	Appraising	Brief
Body language	Impatient	Open	Reserved/ calm	Closed
Voice	Emotional/ direct	Emotional/ lively	Emotional/ calm	Unemotional/ cool
Walk	Energetic/ quick	Energetic/ springy	Little energy/ measured	Little energy/ controlled
Conversation	About results	About people	About the purchase	About details/ facts
Way of listening	Impatient	Digresses	Willing	Selective
Nature	Positive	Friendly	Affirmative	Appraising
Behaviour	Strong ego	Positive/ optimistic	Non- aggressive	Critical/ suspicious
Demanding with regard to	Design/ quality	Colour/ style	Reliability / cost	Technical details
Determination	Decisive	Dynamic	Cautious	Apprehensive
Fears	Wasting time	Insulting someone	Taking risks	Making mistakes
Total				

9:
Preparing for Sales Meetings with Prospects and Customers

When you go into sales meetings, you want your customer to buy. But do you just want them to buy what they need? Or would you like them to:

- Be inspired by your ideas and buy the more complex solution you are going to propose?
- Find your product so good that they allow themselves a little more luxury, a few more extras than they originally planned?
- Buy a product you suggest to them, which is ideally suited to their personality and needs?
- Be left with the feeling that you understand them, so that they will buy from you again?

Best practice selling means understanding your customers and proposing solutions that suit them. To achieve this, you will need to do some thorough preparation. Even Yellow salespeople find it difficult to conjure up well-thought-out, tailor-made solutions out of thin air. What is required is a combination of preparation for negotiations with the specific customer, a good basic knowledge of your product, a clear understanding of the four colour styles and plenty of flexibility. And of course, the most important thing is your own enthusiastic attitude towards the meeting and towards closing the deal.

PLAN FOR EFFECT

Selling is a transfer of enthusiasm from you to your customer! In other words, your positive attitude should rub off on your customer. However, if your attitude and expression reveal that you are not really 100% convinced of the value of your product/service, or that you are not sure whether the customer is really ready to buy, then that attitude, too, will transfer itself to your customer. Research carried out by communications scientists and from the field of neuro-linguistic programming (NLP) shows that the effect you have on other people is determined:

- 58% by your body language (non-verbal communication)
- 35% by the tone of your voice
- 7% by what you actually say – the actual words you use.

Your customer will probably believe (unless they have heard of these findings) that it is mainly your words that influence them. So *what* you say is still important, although *how* you say it is also crucial. Your non-verbal communication, however, is even more important because most people are not aware of the influence of their body language in the communication process.

So plan carefully the effect you will have. Every time you are about to enter into sales negotiations, take a few minutes to consider the following questions:

- What style is my customer?
- What sort of presentation appeals to them?
- Is that the sort of presentation I give?
- How do I want to appear? (What will I and what won't I reveal of myself? What am I going to consciously change to suit my customer?)
- What behaviour could the customer show which is likely to throw me off-balance and make me "lose my cool"?
- How do I plan to react in such situations?

Also consider what exactly you are hoping to achieve in the meeting:

- Are you meeting a new customer for the first time? Then you probably will not close a deal today. The aim is to for you to get to know each other. You will have a first opportunity to find out which colour group your customer might belong to, and you will be starting to establish a basis of trust.

- Will you be talking to a customer you already know because they have contacted you and asked for information on a product? Then your goal will be a comprehensive requirement analysis, aimed at providing the necessary information for your customer. As you are already (more or less) familiar with their colour style, you can prepare for the meeting, by making sure you take along suitable material, setting aside enough time for it and choosing the best location (restaurant, the customer's office, your office, the customer's home). You will also have a chance to test your previous evaluation of the customer and revise it as necessary.

- Is this a follow-up meeting where you will be settling final details and setting the seal on the deal? Imagine everything that might prevent the customer from making their decision, and prepare yourself to take them by the hand and lead them forward if necessary.

The success of your meeting will depend on several factors:
- Your customer's colour style, your style, and your own awareness of how to deal with "difference", if any
- Whether you are following a recognised sales process
- How far you are successful in adapting to your customer's real needs and expectations
- How you leap-frog other potential communications barriers, such as different family background, work experiences, education, age or culture.

REMEMBER YOUR OWN COLOUR TYPE

Be prepared to adapt your style to your customer's style. And you know your own colour style by now. So you are also aware of the sort of behaviour you might display that is likely to rub other colour styles up the wrong way. If your customer does not belong to the same colour group as you, they will probably have difficulties with some of your characteristics. So, before a meeting, always consider where the sticky patches could be, where communication could break down.

Below, we have put together a few tips for each colour style, a few things you should think about before meeting any customer, irrespective of their colour style.

Red salespeople

Try to restrain your own ego a little. Ask your customer what they want. Summarise their statements repeatedly and check with them whether you have understood correctly. But be sure to ask in a way that gives them the feeling that they can say "No" and need not be afraid to explain to you exactly what they mean. In other words: Don't intimidate your customer.

Make use of your natural authority to present your product as an expert and to achieve results, but do not hold a pistol to your customer's head simply because you are convinced that something (that is mostly in your interests) has got to happen now. Use your talent for rapid analysis to help the customer find their own solution. Do not try to force your customer to accept the solution of which you are convinced. You can make mistakes, too. You are not always right. Admit it if you are momentarily at a loss for an answer. It makes you more "human", and it certainly will not detract from your reputation as an expert.

You could also consider whether the following ideas could help you to close the deal:

- Show some emotion. You don't have to throw yourself at your customer, just show warmth and sympathy. Every customer wants to be seen as a human being and not just as a business partner. It is OK to express deeper feelings, especially if it helps to develop a long-term, deeper business relationship. You are also influenced by emotions, even if you don't like to admit it. But showing an emotional reaction in an appropriate situation makes you seem much more authentic and human to your business partners.

- Be prepared to accept the viewpoints of other people without losing sight of your own. Take your customer's strategies and ideas seriously. Try to find a way to bring your own ideas and opinions and those of your customer together.
- Allow sufficient time for each meeting and never cut a discussion short simply because you are getting impatient. Talk about everyday things to create a more relaxed atmosphere.
- Never "push" your customer towards a decision. Your emphasis should be on solving problems and not on closing a deal. Slow down.
- Remember what your body language is saying. Lean back and relax occasionally, smile, nod in agreement, underline your words with open-handed gestures (no shaking your fist!).

Yellow salespeople

No one is capable of just listening for hours. Extrovert behaviour serves its purpose for a while – it can be quite entertaining and impressive for the customers. Your talent for talking is a fantastic tool for breaking the ice and making contact. Your frankness is infectious. But remember to allow your customer an equal chance to show their personality and develop their role in the meeting, or they may believe you are not taking them seriously.

Don't think you are the only one who can be creative: Your customers have good ideas, too. Allow your customer the space and time to present their ideas and opinions. Have faith in the fact that you have just the solution the customer needs at your fingertips. You don't need to talk them into the ground to prove it.

Consider how these tips might help you:

- Keep asking questions. Summarise what your customer has said and check whether you have understood correctly.
- Slow down. Allow your customer just as much time to present their needs and ideas as you allow yourself for your presentation.
- Avoid exaggeration. Sooner or later your customer will notice that you exaggerated. Next time, they will not believe you.

- Speak less and speak more slowly. Be conscious of your breathing. It will make you appear calmer and more self-confident.

- Make sure your body language is consistent with your willingness to adapt to your customer: Look them in the eye, make notes, make sure that your gestures are calm and controlled.

- Do not give your customer the feeling that your friendliness means they can take advantage of you. You don't have to be boring if you are practical. Being more practical could prevent others manipulating you or not taking you seriously.

- Allow others to judge you by your achievements and take this advice on board for yourself. It is a fact that your sales figures are more important to your company than the number of times you have played golf with your customers. Never lose sight of your concrete achievements.

Green salespeople

As a Green salesperson, you have a tendency to let your heart rule your head. This could be a particular problem for customers who are very practical. They will see you as too emotional, too intent on nearness. Your talent for relationships is useful for you when you are building up a warm relationship with a customer, but you should never lose sight of your goal, the task in hand.

The following tips may help you ensure smooth communication. Try them and see:

- Limit the number of your close friendships. It is a fact that you can only maintain a deeper relationship, in which you discuss very personal issues, with a certain number of people.
  Consider who you want to share such a relationship with, and do not expect practically-oriented people to be willing to get into deeper relationships.

- Never give up! If the task gets too much for you, you tend to try to reduce the challenge by making friendly overtures. Putting it negatively, you try to ingratiate yourself. Never lose sight of your business goal.

- Take your bearings from your achievements. Often, Greens dislike being judged by their results, feeling that no one takes into consideration the good relationships they have established with customers. And of course, an excellent customer relationship is an important aspect of your work, but not the most important one. Remember right from the outset that you will be judged by your sales figures, and you should use your sales figures as your own yardstick.

Blue salespeople

Blue salespeople have difficulties getting into conversation with customers and they are often regarded as cold and impersonal. Their reserve is interpreted as a lack of willingness to help or to appreciate their customers' feelings. So your goal should be to curb your desire for control and to allow more feeling into your communication with others.

Think about the following tips and how they might help you:

- Express your feelings. If you radiate far more personal warmth in your relationships, this is bound to have a positive effect in connecting with your customers. If you have had a long and intense business relationship with a customer, it is OK to express deeper emotions like joy or disappointment. If you do so, your opposite number is also free to do so in appropriate situations.
- Let other people know the hopes and expectations you have for a project. It is always motivating for others to be actively involved in a plan or in setting a goal.
- Allow yourself to be drawn into "everyday" conversations. Resist your natural urge to get straight down to business. Take the time to talk about everyday topics in order to create a comfortable atmosphere. Sympathise with the issues that are important to your customer at the moment. You are not likely to become someone's life counsellor or therapist just because you listen to their concerns and show some compassion to them.

Flexibility

No matter what colour type you are, the motto that should encompass every aspect of your pre-meeting sales planning is: "Be flexible!".

Of course, good preparation is important, but if you stick rigidly to your pre-programming, you will look pretty wooden when things do not go as planned. You have to be prepared for the unexpected. Your customer may suddenly display characteristics you have not seen in them before. Perhaps they are not the pure Conductor-type you took them for originally, and now suddenly wants to know a wealth of details, with the result that the meeting lasts much longer than you expected. Apparently, they are more of an Implementor after all. You should be able to adapt to this new-found knowledge in this meeting or the next, providing the customer with the information they need and allowing more time for the meeting. Draw up a plan (particularly important for salespeople with a strong Yellow element), but never cling to it stubbornly (this applies particularly to salespeople with a strong Blue element).

Do you know your product?

Never mind what colour style you or your customer are (just for a minute!) – you will be able to sell only if you know what you are talking about. Until you know your product well yourself, you will not be able to present it convincingly to your customers. Never stop pestering the experts in your company with questions until you really do know all the detail about the product or service that you are selling. Then you will be able to present its advantages to others, and you will be convinced that the price you are asking is justified.

You may have experienced the car salesperson who, in the middle of a test drive, tries out the new car's air-conditioning system. He knows the previous model's air-conditioning system inside out, he explains, but they must have changed something. After fiddling around for some minutes, he manages to find the right setting and proudly shows it to you. But he has not convinced you. Not because there is something wrong with the air-conditioning system – that works perfectly. It is his sales professionalism that was not convincing. Every customer wants to buy from an expert. Don't just act like an expert – be one!

Dynamic Communication

The table following shows you at a glance how to make effective use of the three factors – body language, tone of voice and words – for customers of the different colour types.

Factor	Red customer	Yellow customer	Green customer	Blue customer
Body language: 58%	Be at the ready Lean forwards Direct eye contact Controlled gestures	Move much closer Use touch Relaxed, casual Friendly eye contact Expressive gestures	Be more relaxed Methodical Lean back Friendly eye contact Contained gestures	Keep your distance Stand or sit Firm bearing Direct eye contact Restrained gestures
Tone of voice: 35%	Strong Louder, clear Self-confident Direct	Enthusiastic High and low Modulated Friendly, lively	Warm Gentle Constant Low volume	Restrained Direct Reflective Little modulation
Speed of speech and action	Fast (purposeful)	Fast	Slow	Slow (careful)
Words & content: 7%	Winning Results Now New and unique Challenge	Fun I feel Establish a relationship Recognition Exciting	Step by step Help out Guarantee Promise Exciting	These are the facts Tried and tested No risk Analysing Guarantees

> ## CHECKLIST FOR OPTIMUM MEETING PREPARATION
>
> Keep customer files in which you record not only the results of all meetings with customers but also your personal impressions. Also make a note of which colour group you think your customer belongs to.
>
> Before you go to a meeting with a customer, read through that customer's file card in preparation. However, this does not mean that you should go into the meeting with preconceived ideas!
>
> Gather all the information you can get on your product. Make sure your information is always up-to-date.
>
> Gather all the information you can about your customer, especially if this is a new customer: What is their position within their company? Where did they work before that? Who did they buy from before? Who makes the decisions in their company?
>
> Build up a network of sources of information: colleagues, press spokesmen, journalists, and trainers. This is not about collecting gossip and hearsay but about gathering information on customers that might give you an edge in sales negotiations. With up-to-date information, you will be aware of your customer's expectations and will have all the necessary material with you on your first visit, whereas another salesperson will have to wait until their second visit.

CONCLUSION

If you find out that the person you have an appointment with is one of their company's big decision-makers, don't get cold feet. Accept the challenge! It's the only way to grow! The same applies if you are visiting a customer who has a reputation for being "difficult". You can learn something! Perhaps the insights you have gained in this book will help you to determine why this customer is regarded as "difficult". Perhaps you will not find him or her "difficult" at all! Whatever happens, you have the chance to distinguish yourself with the help of thorough preparation, clear communication and all the fun of a challenge! Do you want to make a name for yourself in the sector? Well then, go out and earn yourself the reputation of a salesperson who is good at cracking those difficult customers!

10:

BE COMPETENT AND SELF-CONFIDENT – DEALING WITH RED CUSTOMERS

Be competent and self-confident – this is rule number one when dealing with Red customers. The strategies described here refer primarily to the Conductor. Depending on how strong your customer's Red aspects seem to be, you can choose to employ all the strategies or pick out individual tips. On many occasions, you may need to mix strategies. We will discuss the mixed types with Red aspects – the Persuader and the Implementor – later. However, depending on the individual customer, you may have to mix your own combination of strategies. Also keep in mind that natural observable behaviour – the SUCCESS INSIGHTS colours – is only one component of a person's personality make-up. The more understanding and experience you gain with the system, of course, the more accurate and successful will be your judgement calls.

These strategies focus on the best way to treat the customer and on giving you ideas on how to adapt your style to maximise the interaction in order to achieve the best possible outcome. Of course, this will be easier or more difficult for you depending on what colour style you yourself are, and so this aspect has also been taken into consideration. At the end of this chapter and in the next three chapters, you will find special tips for each individual colour style to help you ensure smooth communication with your customers.

As a Red salesperson, you will also find in this chapter a summary of strategies you can employ with the four colour styles to help you deal with your customers even more impressively.

ATMOSPHERE

If you are meeting a Red customer in your office, make sure the atmosphere is disciplined and businesslike. It would be better to meet in a conference room than in an office cluttered with piles of documents. Welcome them with a firm handshake, and get down to business after a short introductory sentence. You do not need to waste time on small talk, and you would not receive much of an response if you tried it. The Red customer expects you to behave formally, and will not respect casual clothing.

It would be a good idea to draw up an agenda before the meeting of all the points you want to discuss. But remember, you will not be the one who dictates the course of the meeting. Your Red customer will be in control. And even if it is an unusual role for you: Let them! This does not mean that you have to agree to everything they propose. If you have made a list of points that are important to you, you can bring up these points at an appropriate point in the conversation. In fact, you can have just as much influence on the course of the meeting as your customer, but they will still need to be in the driving seat and you in the background.

Maintain a friendly reserve throughout the meeting. If your customer is friendly too, do not misinterpret this as a sign that you have cracked them and that they are now willing to talk about personal matters. If they want to do so, they will, otherwise you can deal with this customer without any atmosphere of obvious trust between you. It is more important to this customer that you are competent. Cultivate an air of self-confidence, but do not make a point of drawing their attention to any points where you are more knowledgeable about the subject than they are.

You are more likely to be received in a hostile, unfriendly manner than with any of the other colour types. Be prepared for scepticism, a customer with an argumentative disposition, anger, sarcasm or impatience. Refuse to let that throw you off-balance. If it gets too much for you, break off the meeting rather than getting into a debate about appropriate behaviour with your customer.

CHECKLIST:
WHAT YOU SHOULD THINK ABOUT BEFOREHAND

Do not let the customer provoke you, do not take things personally.

Take a clock with you and place it where you can see it at all times.

Draw up a brief time schedule. You could ask your customer how much time they have so that you can plan more effectively.

Find out your customer's title and position in the company so that you can address them correctly.

Make a list of the important points you want to mention.

Call to mind your strong points before you go to the appointment, and be self-confident, even if that is not usually your manner.

PRESENT YOUR PRODUCT CLEARLY AND CONCISELY

You can assume that your customer will have a great interest in new products and innovations. This means that you can present them with every new product you have.

EFFECTIVE PREPARATION

A Red customer is not interested in showy glossy brochures. They want brief, summarised fact sheets. Prepare appropriate material beforehand. Prepare thoroughly so that you can really back up your own offer. Present your facts in a logical sequence. If you skimp on preparation and then have to gloss over points you are not certain of in your presentation because you cannot remember the information, the Red customer will shoot you down in flames. They will not mince their words and will let you know you have been found out. Never claim to know something if you cannot back up your claim when asked a question. If this happens, you will lose all credibility in the eyes of a Red customer. It would be better to admit that you don't have the information but will find out and get back to them on the point.

HOW TO MOTIVATE A RED CUSTOMER

The Red customer will become interested in a deal as soon as they have come to the conclusion that you are their equal. That is why it is so important that you appear competent and self-confident.

They will also be motivated when they see that you are going to leave the buying decision up to them and will not try to influence them. It gives them the feeling that you understand them, even if they will never say as much.

Show them that you respect them and allow them their independence. You should also respect their right to express their opinion openly. Reds sometimes have to let off steam, and they appreciate it when others do not take personal offence.

Show that you are competent

From the very beginning, show that you are competent, otherwise the Red customer will not take you seriously. Present your company and your products as respectable and among the best available. For example:

> *My name is Mark Rothwell, a qualified management and tax expert. My company is one of the largest in Europe. I can offer you a whole range of financial services. Whatever you require in order to realise your goals and your wishes, I am sure I can offer you a suitable investment.*

The Red customer is only prepared to do business with the best, so make no secret of your experience and your talents. Show them that you are an expert, in whatever way you can.

No chat

The Red customer has no interest in chatting. Concentrate on the task in hand, not on the person. You will achieve far more if you keep to the subject of business. The Red customer is not particularly interested in how your other customers use the product – unless one of these customers is a well-known personality or an acquaintance whom they admire. Then, of course, you should definitely mention the fact.

Do not bore your Red customer. Your presentation should not be monotone, your solutions must be intelligent and should not be too traditional. The Red customer needs an intellectual challenge, but purely rhetorical questions from you are not enough. They make them feel you are simply making fun of them. But you can certainly proceed faster than you can with other customers and there is no need to explain simple things. The Red customer will ask if they need something explained.

They will probably interrupt you repeatedly to ask questions anyway. So you should be prepared for this, to make sure it does not fluster you. Take the customer's questions as headings under which you can present a summary of your knowledge on that subject. You should ask your customer questions now and again, too, to give them the chance to talk about their situation. The Red customer is not someone who can listen and remain passive for long.

Stress the alternatives

During your presentation, be fully aware of these three key words: Concise, clear, competent. Show your Red customer plans or diagrams where they can see at a glance what you are trying to tell them. Recommendations, research findings, data, etc do not really interest them. Researching and verifying data are tasks they delegate to members of their staff whom you may have the chance to talk to later. They are most interested in the bottom line, and this is where you should focus your attention.

A Red customer wants to know:

- The most important facts
- Important alternatives and options
- The possible consequences of making a decision in favour of your product/service.

Give them clear information on the available options and the probable consequences. The Red customer likes to have alternatives from which they can choose. Then they can decide, and that is very important for them. If you offer them only one solution, they feel fenced in and will probably think you are not very competent. They may then turn to your competitors to get the options they want and all you may have succeeded in doing is educating them on the alternatives.

The best way for you to present your information is with the positive results and findings clearly in the foreground. For example:

There is no more versatile machine than Model A on the market at the moment. This truck deals with jobs of all sizes in only a fraction of the time that would be needed simply to load most other vehicles. Model B, on the other hand, is a more manoeuvrable and financially more attractive alternative. Its technology, however, is not as sophisticated. I have made a list of the technical and performance data of the two models ...

You should not conceal any disadvantages. However, it is not as important to explain the pros and cons to a Red customer as it would be in the case of a Blue customer, for example. A Red customer prefers to receive a list of points in favour of this or that solution.

When talking about your product, stress all the points that:

- Are of advantage for the customer
- Increase the Red's autonomy, freedom of action and power
- Promise increased prestige.

Speak with confidence

Your Red customer has quite a strong ego. They enjoy the company of people who are as self-confident as they are. They accept them as their equals and test their strength on them. Competition is part of everything, as far as they are concerned. Again and again, they will try to challenge you in their choice of words. But for there to be competition, two have to play the game, and you do not have to take up his challenge. Be strong and convincing without flaring up or becoming aggressive.

Use these tips:

- Use words and phrases such as "results", "the bottom line", "immediately", "quickly", "advantages", "new and unique"
- Avoid rhetorical or leading questions
- Use concrete ("What?") questions, and open questions. Do not use questions that can be answered with a simple "Yes" or "No". Such questions make the Red customer feel as if you are talking down to them

- Summarise and reflect
- Give brief, clear answers
- Use short sentences, not long, complicated ones
- Do not exaggerate
- Ask the Red customer's advice, but be careful not to seem at a loss or in need of help.

Statements to motivate a Red customer

- I'm sure you'll want to try it out. You're just the right person to take full advantage of its possibilities.
- You should never accept a proposition like this immediately, but you are someone who can recognise both the advantages and the disadvantages.
- As soon as you have explained the programme to others, they will have no problem working with it. But its success will be attributed to you, because you are the one who made the decision.
- It's a completely new idea. There's nothing comparable on the market.
- The nice thing about this plan is that you do not necessarily have to execute it all yourself.
- You will soon see that it offers you just what you need.
- What do you need and when?

The quicker, the better

Proceed quickly. You can safely assume that your customer will grasp what you say quickly or will let you know if there is anything they do not understand. Besides, the Red customer does not like to waste time and will be pleased if they can see quick results.

Of course, you should not be in such a hurry that you rush through your presentation or forget important information. Your motto here is: "As short as possible and as long as necessary".

You can be sure of one thing: Your Red customer does not set great store by lists of facts and figures. Pick out the essential points. If they want to know more, they will ask. This is also an excellent opportunity to allow the Red customer to take the initiative, giving them the feeling that they are in command. It goes without saying that you should not take this too far and make them drag every piece of information out of you.

Don't argue with a Red

If the customer raises objections, is surly or cold, stay calm. Do not let them drag you into a fight. Do not take their bait or let them rattle you. Refuse to be provoked and, above all, don't take things personally. Try to understand what is making them cross – ask them, if necessary – and present reasonable arguments. (You can read more in later chapters about how to deal with stressful situations or defensive behaviour with a Red customer).

Let the Red win

Reds are quite susceptible to flattery. Take advantage of this little weakness, without being too blatant, of course, and only if you can do it credibly. Compliments that are completely artificial usually sound just so. But you can flatter their ego a little, a Red will buy it.

Allow them the honour of believing that they were the one who came up with an idea first, even if it was originally yours. Stress how much prestige your product will bring them, how it will allow them to tackle or overcome new challenges and how it will mean increased efficiency levels. These are all things that are very important for their self-image. For example:

> *That is an excellent suggestion. It would combine the efficiency of your existing plant with the technical innovations of our system. You will be the first in your sector to introduce such a plant. I have drawn up a list of the corresponding data, which shows you in black and white what the production capacity of your newly equipped plant would be.*

Body language

Your body language should underline your self-confident manner. Stand or sit straight, look them firmly in the eye. Do not beg for their approval with looks or gestures. Neither should you try to establish an artificial personal contact by means of friendly looks, a slap on the back or similar gestures. Your body language should mirror your attitude of a friendly but firm inner detachment from the Red customer. Emphasise your attentiveness and your respect by listening actively. But try not to reveal any signs of uncertainty. If you get irritated, straighten your back and raise your chin. You will not easily be made to feel inferior in this pose.

When explaining something to your Red customer, lean forwards and underline your words with clear, linear movements. Sweeping gestures and pathos have a negative effect on the Red customer. Your gestures should express clarity, dynamism and control. Your tone of voice should also express self-confidence. Speak in a loud, firm, clear voice.

Closing the deal

You will have to be prepared for some tough bargaining when negotiating prices and terms with a Red customer. You will not need very much time to get to the point of finalising the deal, but it will take all your energy and concentration. With a Red customer, the chances are fairly high that you will be able to close a deal on your first or second meeting if you proceed effectively and impress the customer with your competence and organisation.

Be well prepared for the final phase. Briefly summarise the various options and state what their advantages for the customer are. For example:

> *If we follow Plan A, your investment should have paid for itself within three years due to savings in production costs. This period would only be two years in the case of Plan B, which entails the greater investment ...*

Then leave them to make the decision. Do not recommend one of the solutions as the best. If you did, they will probably reject this very solution just to spite you.

Many different salespeople have told us variations on the following example of a successful deal made with a Red customer:

The customer, David Moore, phones the Mercedes car showrooms because he wants to buy a car. The salesperson, Ian Ring, advises him competently and answers all his questions to his satisfaction. They have discussed price and delivery period. Then David says:

'OK, Ian, I'll take the car.'

'But don't you want to look at it first? We've got one on the forecourt.'

'No. I'll buy it.'

'You're welcome to take it for a test drive. You don't have to make up your mind at once.'

'I said I want the car!'

'Of course, as you wish. I'll draw up the contract of sale.'

In this example, the salesman realised just in time that David Moore was about to withdraw from the deal if he raised any more "objections". It really has been known for Red customers to back out of a sale simply because the salesperson refused to believe that the customer was prepared to buy the car without looking at it or test-driving it. It's the sort of behaviour you have to expect with a Red customer. If they want to buy a product – don't put barriers in their way or make assumptions that they want more time. Just close the sale – quickly!

Follow-up

The most important thing in your follow-up with a Red customer is to honour all your promises. If you agreed to do something by a certain date, you must keep to the deadline. Your Red customer could easily interpret unreliability as a sign of disrespect.

Apart from that, the Red customer does not need any special treatment. They like you to keep them informed of all the latest trends. They want you to inform them immediately of any new developments, because they want their offices, their software or services to reflect the state of the art.

They are usually not interested in personal conversations just for the sake of maintaining the contact, unless you know and get on with them very well, and that can take a long time with a Red customer.

CHECKLIST:
STRATEGIES FOR NEGOTIATING WITH
RED CUSTOMERS

Establishing trust:
Be brief and businesslike
Do not waste time on empty phrases
Do not start personal conversations
Be friendly but professional
Allow them to take the dominant role.

Requirement analysis:
Be self-confident and competent
Get down to business quickly
They know exactly what they need. Listen attentively.

Information:
Present alternative offers
Concentrate on the essential facts
Stress prestige, new challenges, and efficiency.

Closing the deal:
Close the deal quickly
Let them make the decision
Let them win.

How not to do it

What the Red customer definitely does not appreciate is personal chat, superfluous information, repetition, and statements without any new information content. It annoys them to have to deal with salespeople who are ill-prepared and who waste their time needlessly. And they probably will not buy from them if their presentations are boring and do not provide a challenge.

On the other hand, you should never give them the feeling that you know their requirements better than they do. Neither should you force them into the role of the loser, since they cannot handle that. And do not argue with them: You will always lose. A Red customer will also not be happy if you ignore their objections or do not take them seriously. Never make promises you cannot keep.

YOUR CUSTOMER IS A PERSUADER

Let us assume you know that your customer is a Persuader whose Yellow aspects are less dominant than his Red ones. How can you modify your strategy?

Let your personality play a greater role

Take more time for personal conversations and an exchange of information about mutual acquaintances. But make sure you do not lapse into gossip. Talk about people the Persuader holds in high regard and whom they respect as their equals. Alternatively, swap stories about common sporting interests, for example your golf handicap or your last tennis match. When you get to know them better, challenge them to a match and, whatever you do, don't let them win deliberately. They will notice and will feel that you do not consider them as an equal partner.

Make your presentation more lively

Instead of merely presenting facts and confining yourself to the most important findings, you can now range further afield. A Persuader will be more interested in who else is using this product. The examples you give should be those of important people. Your presentation will be more of a discussion, although the Persuader will still be firmly in control. Give them the right cues and see whether they take the bait. For example:

> *By the way, George Graham of XYZ Co uses this system, too. Only the other day, he told me how satisfied he was with it, particularly with its speed.*

If a Persuader wants to know more, they will ask.

Pick up their ideas

To an even greater degree than the Conductor, a Persuader will confront you with their own ideas and expect you to produce a suitable solution. So you can expect to have to come up with a completely new answer. Don't let that put pressure on you. Take the time you need, even if they try to hurry you.

YOUR CUSTOMER IS A IMPLEMENTOR

This customer has Blue characteristics, though the Red elements are still dominant. Your strategy should take these Blue aspects into consideration and address them specifically.

Offer more details and printed material

The Implementor requires even more detailed information, so you should bring with you more detailed printed matter, though not quite as much as you would for a pure Blue type. You can offer the written material and see whether they take you up on it. For example:

> *We commissioned several studies on this hydraulic ramp, and some of our customers have also passed on their observations. We have put all this material together into a comprehensive dossier on the product. I can leave you a copy if you are interested.*

Offer more support for long-term decisions

They may suddenly find it difficult to make up their mind because it is difficult for them to foresee the long-term consequences. When presenting the product to this customer, you need to focus even more clearly on the consequences than with the Conductor. You should also describe the disadvantages in greater detail, so that the customer gets no nasty surprises later.

HOW DO YOU SELL TO A RED CUSTOMER IF YOU YOURSELF ARE ...

... a Red Salesperson?

- If you are a Red type yourself, you should not have any problems with a Red buyer.

... a Yellow Salesperson?

- Do not tell jokes or initiate any small talk yourself. Keep to the subject of business, avoid interruptions and do not waste time.
- Avoid physical contact – do not put your hand on their arm or clap them on the back.
- Set clear deadlines and honour them.
- Stick by your convictions and do not try to agree with everything they say.

... a Green Salesperson (opposite type)?

- Deliver your presentation as confidently as possible – eliminate all waffle.
- Do not allow the self-confident and challenging Red customer to intimidate or browbeat you. Be prepared for their brash manner and firmly deliver the right answers to their questions.
- When analysing their requirements, concentrate on the "What?" and "When?".
- Be a little quicker than usual in everything you do, but do not let them pressurise you.
- Concentrate all your attention on the business in hand. Do not think about your relationship with the Red customer, wonder what they think of you personally or consider what you think of them. This is all irrelevant. The best you can hope for is that your Red customer will learn to trust in your competence, even though they are unlikely to trust you as a person.

... a Blue Salesperson?

- Do not smother the Red customer in facts and figures. Confine yourself to the essentials. Get to the point as quickly as possible and concentrate on closing the deal.
- Do not take the Red's gruff manner personally. Be optimistic and friendly.
- Sell them the most innovative products you have to offer, even if it goes against the grain to do so.

ARE YOU A RED SALESPERSON?

Below you will find a summary of the recommended strategies for dealing with customers of the four different colour styles, if you are a Red sales professional.

Customer's colour style	Red	Yellow	Green	Blue
Introduction	Come straight to the point	Be more sociable and open	Speak more slowly, be open	Be formal Get straight down to business
Asking questions	Be careful not to get into a conflict situation	Ask questions, do not argue. Find out the details	Show interest, ask their opinions and pay attention to their answers	Look for the facts Show that you are an expert
Presentation	Move on with every sign of impatience	Involve the customer	Get feedback and describe the advantages	Display your detailed knowledge of the product
Confirmation	Offer options they can choose from	Make future advantages clear, do not hurry them	Describe the advantages for people	Describe the financial advantages
Follow-up	Clear, concrete ideas and options	A wealth of ideas and a look into the future	Concentrate on advantages for their employees	Present facts and details logically
General	Fast negotiation pace	Be open and enthusiastic	Allow yourself time and show that you are genuinely interested	Be accurate, systematic and well-organised

11:

BE OPEN AND EXPRESSIVE –
DEALING WITH YELLOW
CUSTOMERS

Be amusing and expressive, but never lose sight of the business in hand. This is the golden rule for dealing with Yellow customers. Here, too, you have a wide variety of possible strategies you can apply, depending on how strong the customer's "Yellow aspects" are. We will go into greater detail later on the two combination styles Persuader and Relator (with dominant Yellow aspects). At the end of the section, the Yellow salesperson will find a summary of the best tips for dealing with customers of the four colour styles.

ATMOSPHERE

The customer may very well come to your office or even to your home. Ensure a personal atmosphere from the start. Show them around, introduce them to your colleagues and sit down with them in a comfortable seating group. Offer them a cup of coffee or something else to drink. Or arrange to meet them for a meal in a restaurant. Be generous and pay for their meal. A Yellow customer appreciates such gestures.

Yellows love small talk, entertaining conversation, jokes, personal anecdotes and talking about mutual acquaintances. Allow time to lay the foundation for your relationship.

But even if you are getting on like a house on fire, do not overestimate your relationship with the Yellow customer. A warm and friendly atmosphere is normal for them and does not mean that they particularly favour you or your offer. They will be just as warm and friendly to your competitors. Don't let them get you completely on their side, or you will lose your critical distance and will no longer be able to judge whether the customer is still following you.

CHECKLIST:
WHAT YOU SHOULD THINK ABOUT BEFOREHAND

Be sure you pay the bill the first time you go out for a meal with your Yellow customer. Book a table at a trendy venue, somewhere that's in or at a restaurant where they serve specialities.
Go armed with a couple of good jokes.
Find out whether you and your customer have any mutual acquaintances.
If you know their interests and hobbies, read up on the latest information in newspapers or on the Internet so that you will be able to chat to them about these subjects.
Define your business goal in the negotiations precisely so that you will not lose sight of it.
If you already know them, find solutions that support their ideas.

PRESENTATION

Your Yellow customer is a friendly, open-minded person. They look forward to your meeting and hope you will provide them with some entertainment and variety. The difficulties with this customer will not lie in establishing contact with them. You will do that quickly and easily. The problem will be ensuring that your negotiations do not get stuck in that phase, but that you move on to talking about the business in hand and get down to closing the deal. In most cases, you will not get that far at your first meeting. You will have to invest the time for relaxed conversation and to discuss the customer's wealth of ideas.

CHAT, GOSSIP – AND BUSINESS

Take your time getting down to business. This will be particularly difficult if you are a Blue salesperson. If so, prepare even more thoroughly and see the chat phase as part of the service you are offering. Whatever you do: Listen to your customer, let them tell their anecdotes and add a few of your own. The Yellow customer makes it easy for you: They are happy to have an audience. So if you are not the world's greatest conversationalist and entertainer, just listen appreciatively.

Then, when you do get down to business, try to maintain the friendly tone. The tone of the sales meeting is all-important for the Yellow customer. You will not have to draw up a fixed agenda for your meeting with this customer. Structure is not so important to them. But one thing is very important for you: Don't get carried away! Before or during the meeting, make a note of the points you want to clarify. The greatest challenge for a salesperson facing a Yellow customer is how to pin them down. You will have to strike a delicate balance. On the one hand, you want to fix concrete details, on the other, you do not want to pressurise them or bore them with business. For example:

> *Since you just mentioned your last holiday, we ought to fix a delivery date. You know what it's like in summer. Our technicians all want to jet off to Majorca, so we have to plan the deployment of our team well in advance to ensure that our customers don't have to wait. When exactly do you want to have our system installed?*

BE IN CONTROL OF THE SALES MEETING

You need a firm hand to lead the Yellow customer where you want them to go. Be relaxed, incorporate jokes into your presentation, but be ready to steer the conversation firmly back to the business in hand when your customer digresses. You will have to accept repeated digressions, and you should not interrupt your customer or cut them off too obviously. But you can pick up cues that they give you and use them to guide the conversation back in the right direction. Be in control of the conversation, but take it easy. Make sure you don't seem authoritarian or condescending.

CONTACTS AND RECOGNITION MOTIVATE THEM

Your Yellow customer wants to have fun. That is what motivates them. Allow them the opportunity for self-portrayal, let them tell their jokes while you lean back and enjoy the show. Let them participate in your network if you can. Pick up on their ideas and take them seriously. They may talk a lot, and a lot of what they say may be only hot air, but they really do have some good ideas. These can give you new inspiration. Praise their ideas and also show your appreciation of them by giving them serious thought.

Bring them down to earth

While you analyse their requirements, your Yellow customer is likely to start playing with ideas of how to solve the problem or what the ideal solution could be. Take notes in order to be able to integrate their ideas into your presentation. You can benefit from their creativity. It may help you to come up with a solution that neither of you had thought of. For example:

Your idea sounds excellent, a whole new way of looking at things. No one has thought of that before, so I would like to talk it over with one of our most experienced experts. Would you be interested in putting it into practice? If so, why don't we decide which data is important, and then I would suggest meeting again next Thursday. By then I will have a concrete solution for you.

Of course, it will not be possible to turn all their ideas into concrete solutions, so try to find out by means of skilful inquiry which ideas they are really serious about. If you notice that they are really taken with one of their own ideas, pick up on it and offer them a concrete solution.

The Yellow customer requires a great deal of flexibility and also the tenacity not to get lost in their impractical projects. The Yellow customer is the ideal partner for innovative projects, but you will have to play the role of the realist or pragmatist and leave the creative, imaginative side to them. Again and again, you will have to bring them back down to earth:

Your idea is great. How can we execute it? This is how I see it in practice ...

You will have to learn to accept their volatility and the sometimes chaotic way they explain their requirements or set about finding solutions.

As they are open to everything new, you should offer them your latest products. They will always be enthused about them and willing to give them a try.

Emphasise the prestige

As the Yellow customer is mainly interested in relationships and contacts, you can integrate these into your presentation. Tell them who is already using this product, what their experience has been, how they have applied it, etc. They may know the other customers you refer to and may want to speak to them about the product at a later point. So it follows that you should be careful to mention only customers who you are sure will be happy to pass on their positive impressions of your product. You could also give the Yellow customer a list of references from people they know and respect. For example:

> And I'm proud to say that most of the members of our international football team have chosen this product, including ...

Throw in a few examples from your own experience, if you have used the product yourself. And it is very important to give your customer the chance to add some examples from their own experience. They may have used a similar product or one from your competitors' range. Let them revel in their stories. They love talking about their own exploits.

In addition, emphasise all the advantages of your product that promise popularity and satisfaction: If the product means that your customer can make work easier or more enjoyable for their colleagues, for example (which means they will all be full of praise for them). A Yellow customer likes serving others, and so you should draw particular attention to the aspects of your product that allow them to do just that.

The Yellow customer probably won't find technical details about your product all that thrilling. If it is possible, emphasise the aesthetic aspects, the comfort, and the positive image of your product.

A discussion, not a lecture

The Yellow finds details boring. Do not deliver long speeches but discuss things with them. They need to be able to talk with you, to be active, to put forward their own ideas and, now and again, to tell a story. You can awaken their interest by asking them about something personal. That will make them sit up and take notice. They will be glad that you are showing an interest. So, leave out all unnecessary details. The Yellow customer will make up their mind without knowing every detail of a product.

Be lively

You can also win over a Yellow customer with the help of persuasive body language. Maintain eye contact with them, show your enthusiasm openly, and laugh wholeheartedly at their jokes. Let them glimpse the child in you now and again. Of course, it is up to you to decide whether this is really your preferred style, but you will certainly not make a fool of yourself in a meeting with a Yellow customer if you slap your thighs laughing or bang your fist on the table to underscore a statement. And you will certainly not be getting too close if you occasionally pat their shoulder or touch their arm. So be lively and catch their interest. Use gestures to underline your words and find out whether you have any talent as an actor. The Yellow will always love a good show. But be careful not to exaggerate pointlessly, or your customer will think you are making fun of them.

Don't get side-tracked

Support your customer's ideas and include them in your presentation, but do not let them interrupt you too often. Ask them politely to let you finish what you were saying. You could summarise and reflect on what has been said every now and again so that they know where you are. This will help you avoid getting side-tracked and losing your train of thought. You can support your arguments by choosing particular words:

- Explain the advantages to them with terms like "You will look good", "put you in the limelight", "recognition"
- Use phrases that address their need for contacts and creativity, for example: "Crowds of people", "Your colleagues will love it", "Just imagine", "To pick up your idea ..."
- If possible, avoid asking open questions, or you will get endless answers. Ask concrete questions about the specific things you need to know – especially when you get to the stage

of closing the deal, your questions should be phrased in such a way that your customer can only answer either "Yes" or "No"

- Make sure you do not pause for too long in your presentation, or they will jump in and change the subject completely.

Statements to motivate a Yellow customer

- If you draw a comparison with as many other products as I have, the decision is easy.
- I am sure you would like to be able to delegate more tasks to others. This programme allows you to do just that.
- A lot of people know that there is a need for a solution to this problem. But someone has to be the first to try it. However, I'm sure your instincts are sound.
- Combine these ideas and your success so far, and you have the ideal preconditions for a profitable future.
- This is a chance to try something new that will surpass even your present success.
- I will briefly outline the programme to give you an idea of its advantages.

One eye on the clock

Allow yourself enough time to discuss the Yellow customer's ideas with them. But do not let the meeting drag on for hours. You will have to set a time limit, as your Yellow customer never watches the time and does not expect other people to do so. So you should have one eye on the clock. You will reach a point where the result of your meeting will be no better for spending another two hours in discussions – you have achieved all you can in that meeting. For example:

> *I would love to carry on discussing this with you, but unfortunately I have another engagement this afternoon. I'm sure there is someone waiting for you, too. Let's continue our discussion over a beer sometime and, for today, let's just summarise what we have agreed on so far. I have made a few notes and I'll e-mail them to you tomorrow ...*

However, it may be that you will close the deal quite quickly. Be prepared for anything. For example, the customer may arrive much too late because he got stuck talking somewhere else. The Yellow customer is unpredictable. Something is always likely to crop up. You have to be flexible if you want to do business with them.

Be on your guard

Don't take your Yellow customer's enthusiasm at face value. You will avoid disappointment if you are always a bit sceptical of a Yellow customer. You should not let them see this, it is simply a warning to you to question their enthusiasm. There may still be doubts in their mind in spite of their enthusiasm and verbal agreement. Keep asking. Weed out those doubts by digging deeper!

Closing the deal

Once you can see what the possible deal might be, start finalising the details. You might not close the deal at your first meeting. If you do not, take notes during the meeting, write them up later and send them to the Yellow customer as a sort of intermediate report. You should be sure to take this report with you to your next meeting and go through it with your customer, or you will have to start all over again from scratch.

However, the Yellow customer is often unpredictable with regard to the moment when they are ready to close the deal. They can sometimes make their decision on a purely emotional level. If they are enthusiastic, they will agree to buy on your first visit. You can encourage a quick closing of the deal if you can present the Yellow customer with some recommendations from celebrities or people they know. For example:

> I was chatting to Harry Kinsella recently. He installed this system at MICRA a year ago and is absolutely satisfied with it. He liked the price, too, and it is just as good value today.

Statements like these make a strong impression on Yellow customers. Offering incentives for a quick deal is another way to encourage a Yellow customer to make up their mind. Offer them a special discount for the risk involved. Set down all the details in writing so that each party knows exactly where it stands and what its obligations are.

A good example of how to sell successfully to Yellow customers is the story about the "magic place":

A car showroom in America was selling enormous numbers of a particular model they had displayed in the window. No one could really explain the great success of this particular model or why there should be a sudden demand for it. Then the sales manager noticed that the car was displayed opposite a mirror. When a customer got into the car, they could see their own reflection in the mirror! For Yellow customers, this was the factor that prompted them to buy in the end. They could see how good the car looked "on them"!

So, if you sell cars, you should always let your Yellow customer take a test drive. When they see their reflection in the windows of a skyscraper, they are far more likely to buy the car. The same applies to other products: Try to hold up a mirror (real or metaphorical) in which the Yellow customer can see how well the product suits them.

Irrespective of whether you have finalised a deal or not, always end your meeting with a Yellow customer with some personal small talk.

Plenty of follow-up

The Yellow is not a loyal customer – they are too easily tempted for that. If one of your competitors arouses their enthusiasm, they will buy from them. That is why it is particularly important for you to offer a good, constant follow-up service. Keep in touch, chat to your customer, and keep inquiring whether they need anything. In this way, you will learn immediately if they require a product you can offer them.

CHECKLIST:
STRATEGIES FOR NEGOTIATING WITH YELLOW CUSTOMERS

Establishing trust:
Be sociable and entertaining.
Offer contacts.
Be flexible.
Accept their volatility.

Requirement analysis:
Let them play with ideas.
Always come back to a concrete situation.

Information:
Avoid giving too many details. Mention only the essential points.
Introduce them to new products.
Emphasise prestige and references.

Closing the deal:
Be persistent in negotiating the conditions.
Offer incentives.
Record everything in writing.
Offer plenty of follow-up.

How not to do it

If you leave the decisions up in the air, you will never get the deal done, so don't wait for the Yellow customer to make a decision. Take the initiative and get down to brass tacks.

You should be careful not to kill their creativity and *élan* and, especially, you should not tell them what to do. Yellows do not like rules, and are more likely to do the opposite out of defiance.

If you do not want your Yellow customer to go looking for a friendlier salesperson, you should not be curt, cold, silent or arrogant. It should also be clear to you that with this customer, you will not be able to concentrate purely on the business in hand. Your attention will be fixed mainly on your customer as a person. Avoid being too practical, do not rush off as soon as you have the contract in your pocket.

YOUR CUSTOMER IS A PERSUADER

You have noticed that your customer talks a lot and jumps from one subject to another in a chaotic manner but that, at the same time, they know more or less exactly what they want. Also, the customer interrupts you again and again in a somewhat dominant manner, and takes over the conversation themselves. By  the look of it, they have fairly strong Red aspects. How will you deal with that?

References from important people
Make sure that you provide references from people whose standing is equal or superior to that of your customer. Refer to their competitors and stress how your product will give them a competitive edge.

Think of results
Move towards closing the deal with greater speed than you would with a purely Yellow customer. The Persuader is far more aware of the time factor. Try not to steer the conversation too obviously, they may not want to be led by you. Keep summarising the results and benefits from using your product/service. They may be more likely to finalise the deal first

time around, since results are more important to them than to a
pure Yellow customer. The Persuader demands a high degree of
flexibility from you, because it will take you a while to find out
how "Red" they are and to decide whether they want to take
control of the negotiations or leave it to you to steer them towards
closing the deal.

Your Customer is a Relator

Your customer is interested in
establishing as many contacts as
possible, but you can also sense a real
personal interest in you. They may
have a Green element in their make-up
that you can adapt your strategy to
suit.

Add a personal element
Reveal some personal details about
yourself or your family if the
opportunity arises. You could even inquire about your customer's
private life, if appropriate. In your presentation, you can
emphasise what advantages the product would have for your
customer personally, for their family or colleagues. These are
things that are important to them.

Ensure that they can sense your personal regard for them and
that you want to win their trust.

Emphasise security and reliability
In addition to their enthusiasm for all things new and their wealth
of ideas, the aspect of security will always be important for this
Green-Yellow. Will your product offer them security? Emphasise
the reliability of your product and your company. Show them that
your company is a competent and reliable business partner with
whom they can achieve their ideas. For example:

We have 50 years' experience with systems of this kind and have successfully tailored many products to the requirements of our customers. I am sure that our technicians will put your excellent idea into practice in such a way that you will be able to depend upon it for many years to come.

Be persistent when it comes to achieving results

On the one hand, the Relator displays the grasshopper mind of the Yellow type. On the other, they have the typical Green problems in making a decision. This makes it even more difficult for you to achieve concrete results and to "help" your customer to close the deal. Offer them incentives that might prompt them to make up their mind, and keep inquiring what else needs clarification to enable them to choose your product. However, do not become impatient or they will not voice their misgivings. Go into their doubts in detail and be sure to leave no question unanswered.

HOW DO YOU SELL TO A YELLOW CUSTOMER IF YOU YOURSELF ARE ...

... a Yellow Salesperson?
- You should not have any particular problems. Just one thing: Don't forget to ask them to fill out the order form.

... a Red Salesperson?
- Be a bit more friendly than usual and not quite so businesslike.
- Be more tolerant and not too critical of their suggestions. Take up their suggestions and do not dictate the solution you imagined to be the best.
- When you have closed the deal, ask them once more for their opinion. This is good for your relationship.

... a Green Salesperson?

- Overcome your mistrust and your inner resistance to the Yellow's over-enthusiastic manner. Then you will have no problems with them. You do not have to become their friend.
- Step up your pace somewhat, but do not let them fluster you, even if they jump from one subject to another. Insist again and again, but in a friendly manner, that you return to the business in hand.

... a Blue salesperson (opposite type)?

- Do not expect the Yellow customer to absorb all the facts and figures you present. Concentrate on the most important points, fix your attention on "Who?" and "What else?" when you are analysing their requirements.
- Show a willingness to discuss ideas with them, even if you are not absolutely certain that they are viable propositions.
- Be as friendly as possible.
- Offer your most innovative products.
- Offer speedy follow-up to prevent the Yellow customer buying elsewhere. As your reticent manner makes you the type of salesperson with whom they have the greatest problems, they are the type of customer you will most easily lose to your competitors.

ARE YOU A YELLOW SALESPERSON?

If you are a Yellow sales professional, the table below is a summary of important strategies you can use with the four colour styles.

Customer's colour style	Red	Yellow	Green	Blue
Opening	Not too relaxed, be businesslike	Force yourself to keep to the agenda	Slowly, slowly, don't be too direct References work best!	Slowly, do not be too direct or open Try to be more formal
Asking questions	Work at the customer's pace Beware of impatience Direct questions	Take notes They will forget to do so Informal open questions	Cautious, tactful questions Subjects related to people Listen to the answers	Take notes Proceed methodically and in a structured manner Structured questions
Presentation	Do not digress Give benefit/ outcome statements	Enjoy the presentation, make it entertaining and smooth	Support your statements with references	Provide proof of your statements Show you know your product well
Confirmation	Present options and leave everything else to the customer	Share their dreams and don't push them to make a decision	Reduce the risks, give personal assurances	Present the logical alternatives
Follow-up	Support their aims	Summarise agreements in writing	Show them that their position in comparison to others will be strengthened	Do not forget any details, facts, figures or prices
General	Be precise, efficient, organised and impersonal	Be relaxed, but make sure you get the job done	Take a sympathetic attitude	A difficult customer Be prepared

12:

Winning Trust –Dealing with Green Customers

Once you have won a Green customer's trust, you have as good as got the contract in your pocket. And you will have won a loyal customer who will not desert you easily. There are a few special points to be observed with Relators and Co-ordinators, which are described in this chapter.

Atmosphere

Your Green customer needs to trust you before they will do business with you. The physical surroundings in which you have your sales meeting with a Green customer and the "nice" atmosphere you receive them in are especially important. They appreciate it far more than the other three colour groups if you greet them in a friendly manner and if they can sense your interest in them. For example:

> *Well, thank you for having this meeting, and I would be glad to advise you on your financial affairs insofar as I can. I hear you are looking for a safe long-term investment. Perhaps you would like to tell me first exactly what you have in mind, and then I am sure we can find the right investment for you. We can take as much time as you like, so that you can get to know me better and trust me. Most of my clients have been coming to me for financial advice for many years.*

The initial phase in which a basis of trust is established takes longer with the Green customer than with the other colour groups. You should invest enough time and attention to make this possible. Create a relaxed atmosphere if you meet the customer in your own office. You can win them over if you are willing to reveal something of yourself as a person: Tell them how you started out in this company, show them a photograph of your family or explain to them why you have chosen to hang a particular picture on the wall. Your Green customer wants to know what sort of person you are, so they like to hear personal details from you.

However, it is more likely that they will invite you to their office or to their home. They feel happiest and safest within their own four walls.

CHECKLIST:
WHAT YOU SHOULD THINK ABOUT BEFOREHAND

Allow enough time in your schedule.
Allow your customer to choose where you meet. Indicate your willingness to visit them in their office or at home.
Draw up a list of your (Green) customers who have already used the product successfully. Ask them in advance whether this Green prospect can get in touch with them later.

PRESENTATION

You will find a friendly, somewhat reserved customer who would like to be your friend. Their reserve is not a sign of distrust, but of hanging back until they find out what sort of person you are.

WIN THEIR TRUST

Start the conversation with personal remarks. If you do not know the customer yet, tell them something about yourself, stressing your qualities as a person rather than as an expert in your field: Tell them why you enjoy selling your products and why you enjoy working as a salesperson. If this is not your cup of tea, think of something else about yourself you can tell them. It is important that they get to know you as a person and that you are prepared to reveal something of yourself. And allow them the chance to do the same. Ask them about their interests and lifestyle. Talk about their family or hobbies. Look for common ground. For example:

> *This estate car is just the right size for you and your family. There's enough room for your whole family and all your holiday luggage. Friends of mine have got three children like you and they recently went on holiday to the South of France. They were very pleased with the car, because it was so roomy and comfortable.*

Take a human interest and show that this interest is sincere, that you are not only there to sell them something.

If you ask these questions just to get through the sales process and don't really listen to the answers, they will notice it. And then the result will be the opposite of what you intended. They will think that you are only interested in business and are not prepared to listen to their specific requirements. Greens sense very quickly whether a salesperson is being honest. They sense every false note. So, even if a relationship of trust between yourself and your customer does not seem to you to be the most important thing, and if you are normally more practically-oriented, accept the fact that a Green customer sees things differently. For this customer, the phase of establishing trust counts for more than the usual 40%, so work hard to earn their confidence and his friendship.

You can also convince them that you are trustworthy by providing them with genuine references from other customers, preferably from other Green customers this Green customer knows. They should be people they are familiar with, whom they have had contact with for years or frequently do business with.

HOW DO YOU MOTIVATE A GREEN CUSTOMER?

If your Green customer senses that they, as a person, are important to you, this gives them a strong motivation to do business with you, so show an interest in them as a person and demonstrate that you remember what they have told you in the past. For example:

> Let me see if I can summarise your main requirements. Your aim is to retire at 55 with an income that enables you to maintain more or less your present standard of living. You want to put your two children through university and to have enough money for a nice holiday trip every year. Your hobby, gliding, is quite expensive. This is just the right moment to start planning your finances and choosing a safe investment.

Reveal some private details about yourself. Show your customer that you are interested in a long-term business relationship – but, again, only if this is really true. Otherwise, they will notice that you are being insincere.

Another way to motivate this customer is to state clearly when you are of the same opinion as they are. That does not mean that you must agree with everything they say, but if it so happens that they express an opinion you agree with, tell them so.

Honesty is very important to a Green customer. If they see that you are not hiding anything, that you also draw their attention to possible disadvantages and speak your mind openly, they will trust you and be willing to do business with you. It is also important for them to feel accepted by you, so you should consciously provide plenty of reassurance and respect – even if for you, it seems perfectly obvious that you take them seriously.

Precise requirement analysis

For the Green customer, a needs analysis is almost as important as establishing a basis of trust. Ask them exactly what they want and listen attentively. Familiarise yourself with their situation until you are sure you know exactly how they would like to use your product and where the problems lie. Ask questions that refer to their personal views or business goals. Keep asking until you know what and how they think.

Don't stop until you have a really detailed picture of the situation. It may be that you think you know pretty early on in the talks what it is your customer needs. However, with this customer, you should not rely on your instincts – instead you should test your assumptions. You will be killing two birds with one stone: Your customer will be impressed that you are paying them such a great deal of attention – this will strengthen your relationship. At the same time, by asking so many questions, it will be easier for you to find a tailor-made solution for your customer. These two factors mean that they will find it much easier and much less daunting to close the deal than it otherwise might be.

Offer tried and tested products

The Green customer tends to stick to tried and tested solutions, to products they have already used and are happy with. They won't try innovative products until others have tested them sufficiently first – in other words, when they are no longer innovative. So you should offer them your well-established, standard products and solutions. If the customer is not yet familiar with them, be sure to supply plenty of evidence and statistics of their reliability in use. Your material must satisfy their need for security and emphasise factors that show that they are not taking any risk buying these products. That is why references or reports from other reliable customers are a good means of inspiring a Green customer's trust in your product. However, the references must be from people they trust.

Image, prestige and outward appearances are not particularly important to the Green customer. They want a reliable product that meets their expectations and is of high quality. They do not need others to admire them for being the first to try out something new or because they have bought a particularly amusing/attractive/original product. Instead, they want their colleagues to admire them for having made a sensible, logical decision and chosen what is generally acknowledged to be a good product.

Key factors: Security and time

You will have realised already that you have to give a lot of time for a Green customer. But they are worth it, because once you have won their confidence, they will be one of your most loyal customers. The more often you do business with them, the quicker they will be to close the deal with you, simply because they have been so satisfied with your service in the past.

Once you have found out what they need, you can present your proposals, and you should continue slowly and carefully. Do not overwhelm them with the force of your arguments, inquire every now and again whether everything is clear or whether they have any questions. It is up to you to grasp the initiative and ask. Greens often do not admit their uncertainty openly. They tend to wait and see. So you should encourage them to ask questions. Eye contact will often reveal whether a Green customer is still following your presentation or whether there is a problem. If they no longer look you in the eye, you should ask whether they would like you to explain something in greater detail.

Maintaining eye contact, that is looking your Green customer directly in the eye, also adds to your powers of persuasion.

As security is a priority for them, emphasise all the advantages of your product that guarantee low risk, durability and stability of value. Go into these in great detail, and repeat yourself if necessary. If the Green's family stands to profit from your product, make a special point of drawing their attention to this benefit. Where their family is involved, the Green is quite capable of making decisions on an emotional level.

Whatever you do, remain patient and give your customer time. If you proceed too quickly and put them under pressure, you will lose their goodwill and trust.

Doubts

A Green customer will listen attentively to you and if they like it, they will support your presentation with nods and words of agreement. However, do not take their willingness to listen to you as a sign that they are satisfied. Their friendly manner does not mean that they think everything is wonderful. The Green customer has difficulty expressing their misgivings. They are keen to maintain a harmonious atmosphere and do not want to spoil things by saying something negative about your product. So be particularly watchful for unexpressed objections. The Green customer needs a lot of encouragement before they will express their doubts, and needs confirmation from you that it is OK for them to do so, that you will not take things personally. For example:

> *I'm getting the feeling that you are a bit doubtful about this aspect of the product, and I would like to know exactly where your misgivings lie. Comments like these from our customers help us in the further development of our products and ensure that we keep up with the latest technological standards. So please do not hesitate to express your doubts. I really would like to hear them.*

The Green customer's behaviour here is hardly surprising when you consider that they tend to take criticism of their work personally.

If you have differing views on a question, these should certainly be discussed and if possible clarified. Your aim should be to reach agreement on as many points as possible, as this gives your Green customer a positive feeling. They like to feel that you also think the solution is right, and not just them. However, if you agree "opportunistically", you will lose all credibility. If you yourself have doubts, you should also voice them and not suppress these views just to preserve harmony.

It is important not to hurt their feelings. So whatever you do, do not gloss over any of your customer's misgivings and pass them off as unimportant. If your customer sees them as a problem, then you should not ignore them.

Devote a lot of time, patience and care to the clarification of any problems. In the end, this will enable the customer to close the deal quicker. You may have to visit the customer several times to provide confirmation before they will sign the contract of sale.

Ask questions, listen and subtly take the lead

Asking questions and listening play a very important part in your presentation technique. Ask concrete questions, be relaxed and informal. When you are explaining something, take frequent pauses for thought. Do not deliver a monologue. Instead, limit yourself to shorter explanations and allow the customer more time to ask questions or express their opinion. Offer them reasoned opinions rather than options. If you offer this customer alternatives, you are more likely to confuse him. In contrast to the Red customer, they do not like making decisions and, if they have to choose between two alternatives, both of which sound good, they will be afraid of making the wrong decision. You can prevent this situation by presenting only one solution that you work out in more and more detail together with the customer.

Whatever you do, do not put your Green customer under pressure. Do not drive them forward with open-and-shut questions. Support them cautiously but firmly in their decision-making. The Green customer will not take over the leadership of the sales meeting, but you should not lead or push him too openly either.

Use soothing expressions such as "think it over", "that is a great help for both of us", "guarantee", "rely on me", "step by step".

Statements to motivate a Green customer

- I have the impression that this is the right product for you. I can warmly recommend it.
- It is important to maintain the same standard as the others.
- Why don't you call a few people who had to make the same decision. I have a list of customers who I am sure would be glad to share their experience with you.
- I am sure you don't want change for change's sake. Your system is very effective, and this would make it even more so.
- I would be happy to drop by and show you how I personally work with this system. Then we could talk about all your other questions.
- The main focus in this system is on security. It offers greatly improved security for you and your family.
- A lot of companies are using this system already. Here is a list. I would be glad to give you a few names of people you could contact.
- Take your time and think it over before you make up your mind.

Closing the deal

The Green customer probably won't agree to buy on your first meeting, even if you have convinced them. They need time to think about the deal after you have left, when you can no longer influence them. They may also want to discuss the matter with colleagues so that they do not have to bear the responsibility of the decision alone.

You can influence them positively in this phase by giving them special guarantees for the product. For example:

> In our experience, there are so few problems with this machine that we can give a guarantee of up to four years on all parts. And if a problem should occur, just phone me and I'll take care of it personally.

This will increase their confidence in the quality of the product, and they will give you credit for accepting and taking into account their need for security.

To return to our example of the car showroom: Car salespeople say that a Green customer likes to buy a car they have driven before, and the best thing would be for no one to notice that they have a new car. The most persuasive arguments for the Green customer are:

> *It's the same well-established model you already know. The same make, almost the same equipment, the same performance. They have only made a few cosmetic changes. If you like, I can order it in the same colour as your old one. Your neighbours won't even notice you've got a new car.*

Follow-up

If you have given your Green customer a promise, you must keep it. Otherwise they will see it as a sign that you do not regard them highly enough, that they are not important enough to you.

Keep in touch with this customer. Call them, ask them how they are. Do not call them specifically and only to find out whether they need anything from you, make it a more personal call: You had not heard from them in a while, so you decided to telephone. You should give them the feeling that the main focus is not on business, but on them as a person, on their well-being. Then you can also ask, by the way, how they are getting on with the last product they bought from you and whether there is anything you can do for them. In this way, you will find out whether they have any unforeseen problems with the product or if they are unhappy with it for some reason. The Green customer does not like making complaints, so they will be glad you asked.

The Green customer will become angry if guarantees are not honoured or promises are not kept. They have a memory like an elephant and are not likely to forget in a hurry. They will hesitate, but they will stubbornly demand their rights. And so it is important that you should take over the reins when something has gone wrong. The Green customer will always understand your situation if you explain to them the reasons for faults or problems. They just do not want to be ignored or neglected.

CHECKLIST: STRATEGIES FOR NEGOTIATING WITH GREEN CUSTOMERS

Establishing trust:
Earn their trust.
Visit them repeatedly.
Tell them something about yourself.

Requirement analysis:
Proceed slowly and cautiously.
Check with them frequently, discuss with them.

Information:
Present facts and figures.
Stress the personal advantages for them.
Put particular emphasis on the security and lasting value of the product, where applicable.

Closing the deal:
Give them time.
Lead them carefully towards closing the deal, take the initiative.
Tempt them with special guarantees.

How not to do it

If you are not honest and make claims you cannot back up and which later turn out to have been exaggerated or untrue, you will lose this customer's trust. They will also "clam up" if you rush or pressurise them. Do not force them to act quickly, that is tantamount to an open invitation to say "No". Do not treat them condescendingly and do not pass off their need for security as unimportant. That's the way they are, and you will not change them. You will only lose their custom.

Your Green customer will also take offence if you treat them too impersonally and only concentrate on business. They never do business on any scale with someone they do not know personally.

When they describe their requirements or give you their opinion on your proposal, do not interrupt. A Green customer is very sensitive when they sense that you may be about to "debate" with them or not take them seriously.

YOUR CUSTOMER IS A RELATOR

Your customer is a "Green", but they are still very open-minded and ready to give new things a try. So, take their "Yellow corner" into consideration and integrate the corresponding components into your strategy.

Take their ideas seriously

Encourage them to express their ideas and show them that you are competent enough to take up their ideas and integrate them into the overall concept. The Relator may not take the initiative and volunteer their ideas. Ask them about their ideas and take them seriously. And if you can really help them to find a specific and personal solution on the basis of their own idea, you will probably have won a life-long customer.

Proceed more quickly

The Green-Yellow Relator probably needs less time than the pure Green customer to absorb your presentation and to make up their mind. Challenge them a little, without hurrying them. You can try to speed things up a little.

Offer them contacts

The Relator is not absolutely intent on making new contacts, but if they have strong Yellow aspects in their make-up, they will be interested in business contacts. So draw their attention to your references, tell them what's new in the industry or find out whether you have mutual acquaintances. It will be easier to find references for them, as you can also put them in touch with Yellow types.

YOUR CUSTOMER IS A
CO-ORDINATOR

Does your customer ask a lot of detailed questions? Are they interested in printed matter? And yet you are still sure that they are a Green customer? Then you are dealing with a Co-ordinator whose Green aspects are dominant. However, you can deal with them even more effectively if you also take their Blue aspects into consideration.

Answer all their questions

Do not become impatient if they ask you a lot of questions. Answer them all in detail until they are satisfied. Listen attentively, because the Co-ordinator will voice their doubts very diplomatically. Take them seriously and inquire again until you really have dispelled all doubt. This customer, too, will reward your patience and willingness to take them seriously with loyalty.

Keep a bit more distance

Leave it to the Co-ordinator to decide how close they want your personal contact to be. When you sense the limits they set, accept them. They are more reserved and suspicious than a pure Green customer, and it will take you longer to warm to them.

How do You Sell to a Green Customer if You Yourself Are ...

... a Green salesperson?

- On the whole, you will not have any problems.
- However, remember that your customer, like yourself, needs security, so make sure you provide it. Do not let them see your own insecurity. Be as confident as possible.

... a Red salesperson (opposite type)?

- Proceed more slowly than usual and devote a lot of time to the phases of establishing trust and requirement analysis.
- Do not dismiss the Green's need for security. Do not treat them condescendingly and press them to buy something just because you think it is the best solution. Your Green customer has to reach this conclusion themselves. You can only support them.
- Proceed more slowly than usual, offer more details.
- Be friendly and show your regard for them as a person.
- Do not lay too much emphasis on new and innovative products.

... a Yellow salesperson?

- Do not be too effusive and hearty before it is clear that they have confidence in you and that they like you.
- Stick to the facts and figures. No exaggeration.
- Your ability to make contacts will make it easier for them to place their trust in you. But above and beyond that, the Green customer expects a great deal of information about the product you are selling.

.... a Blue salesperson?

- Give them time to digest all the facts.
- Chat about your families, tell them something about yourself, and be friendly at all times.

ARE YOU A GREEN SALESPERSON?

In the table, you will find important strategies you can employ with the four colour styles if you are a Green salesperson.

Customer's colour style	Red	Yellow	Green	Blue
Opening	Be direct and confident Do not waffle or hesitate	Be sociable and friendly	Establish trust and friendship	Be more formal and less open
Asking questions	Beware of impatience and follow their pace	Make notes and go into detail	Allow plenty of time to think problems through	Ask detailed, practical questions, be logical
Presentation	Be well-organised and businesslike Look professional	Be entertaining, enthusiastic and swift Tell stories	Mention references from customers	Produce evidence to support your statements and show your product knowledge
Confirmation	Make the alternatives clear	Fix your attention on future advantages and increased prestige	Give personal assurances	Name the logical alternatives
Follow-up	Show options with good chances of success	Show how ideas and dreams can be realised	Show the added advantages for this relationship	Be detailed and businesslike
General	Concentrate on facts, not feelings	Be direct but empathetic	A slow, informal talk	Be well-prepared

13:

HAVE ALL THE DETAILS – DEALING WITH BLUE CUSTOMERS

You will need a plentiful supply of three things when you visit a Blue customer: Time, patience and printed material. If you fulfil these conditions, you will conform precisely to their expectations and have a good chance of closing the deal successfully. At the end of this chapter, you can also read how to modify your strategies to suit a Co-ordinator or an Implementor (with dominant Blue aspects).

ATMOSPHERE

A Blue customer likes to keep their distance, both physically and emotionally. They are not interested in revealing any personal details, nor do they want to hear anything personal about you. If you respect this, they will be willing to do business with you.

When you enter their office, you will find a formal, businesslike atmosphere. Your Blue customer will greet you politely, but coolly and with reserve and get down to business straight away. Do not try to break the ice you think you can feel by striking up a relaxed, chatty conversation – that will not melt the ice. Your customer will only warm to you if you get down to business and let your professional competence speak for itself.

So don't take the impersonal atmosphere personally. This will be difficult for you, particularly if you are a Green or Yellow salesperson. But the best thing you can do is to see everything on a purely business level and forget the emotional level completely. When you have visited this customer many times, you may be able to establish something akin to a personal relationship. But that is not essential for you to close the deal successfully. And closing the deal successfully is the most important thing for you – and for your Blue customer, too.

In the first few minutes, or during your first meeting with a Blue customer, your competence is what it's all about. The customer wants to know: "Is it worth getting into lengthy discussions or not?" So concentrate on showing yourself at your most competent. Send them some printed matter before your first visit so that they can read something about your company and you. For example, you could start by saying:

> *I am a qualified management expert and tax expert. I am sure you will have read about my professional background in the dossier I sent you. I have 14 years experience in financial consultancy, and I keep abreast of all the latest developments. This means that I know my way around the jungle of constantly changing legislation in this sector and I am pleased to place my knowledge at your disposal.*

Be careful to be sincere and do not exaggerate. The customer may make a note and come back to it at a later point, so you should be able to stand over everything you say.

**CHECKLIST:
WHAT YOU SHOULD THINK ABOUT
BEFOREHAND**

Allow yourself enough time, do not make any important appointments after this one to ensure that you do not have to break off the sales meeting in a hurry.
Send them some material about yourself, your company and the product in advance.
Draw up a precise plan of action.
Plan corresponding written material for every point in your presentation and arrange it in the correct order.
Fill in the gaps in your own knowledge: Have your company's experts give you detailed information on the product.

PRESENTATION

While you are talking, there will probably be frequent pauses where the customer falls silent because they are thinking. Don't let their silence, suspicion or critical questions bother you. You will have to put up with them if you want to do business. And the better you do this, the sooner you will be closing the sale.

LISTEN ATTENTIVELY

Analysing the customer's requirements gives you the chance to find out exactly where a deal between you and this customer might fall through. Allow them to describe their requirements in detail and tell you how exactly they plan to use your product. Ask targeted questions to find out exactly which points are important to them. You may have to sit down with one of your company's experts and work out a tailor-made solution and, to do this, you will have to be able to describe to the expert exactly what the customer needs. So make detailed notes – the more complex the solution the customer wants, the more comprehensive your notes should be. Your Blue customer will appreciate it when they see that you are trying to understand their situation. However, do not expect them to express their feelings. The most they will do is praise your competence or methodical manner.

If you are planning a large-scale deal with them or if the solution is very complex, it would be better to separate the presentation and the requirement analysis, thus giving you the opportunity to prepare yourself and to bring with you the appropriate written material. For example:

> *Mr Miller, I have made detailed notes of your requirements. I would like to work out a solution that is tailored exactly to your needs. To do so, I will need time and the professional know-how of our experts. After all, we want a solution that will satisfy your high standards. And so I would suggest that we make an appointment next week when we both have enough time and when I can present you with a sophisticated, well-rounded offer.*

You should move on to the presentation straight after the needs analysis only if you are absolutely sure that you are prepared for delivering an *ad hoc* talk. Be self-critical and measure your knowledge by the customer's yardstick: "Can you really tell them everything they need to know?" If not, do not settle for less than your best. Make a new appointment, prepare yourself thoroughly and then deliver an impressive and masterly presentation.

WHAT YOU CAN PLAN

Above all, your presentation should be logical and well-structured. It is absolutely essential to bring the Blue customer some printed material to support your presentation. Ensure that its order mirrors that of your presentation. A Blue customer will become irritable if they have to keep turning the pages looking for the right material.

You should also send him in advance detailed written information preparing them for your presentation.

Draw up an agenda and stick to it. If your customer has drawn up their own agenda, use that and incorporate your points discreetly at suitable moments.

To be well-prepared, consider beforehand what objections or questions your customer might have. If this is a very important deal, talk through your presentation with colleagues to help you detect any weak points.

Think whether you know other Blue customers who might be willing to give you references beforehand. Only these references will be acceptable to the Blue customer.

How do I Motivate a Blue Customer?

The greatest source of motivation for the Blue customer is plenty of detailed material that you leave with them so that they can study it at leisure. Do not hurry them, agree a date when you can meet again and allow them the time in the interval to think things over.

Absolutely exact and 100%

Offer your Blue customer only well-established products and solutions of whose quality you are personally fully convinced. Leave your new, untested products in your office, your Blue customer will not want to try them.

Your presentation should be very precise and pragmatic. Go into detail, and present various possible solutions with their advantages and disadvantages. For example:

> *Let me demonstrate step-by-step how the sensors are positioned in this special version. May I suggest that you take detailed notes of the individual steps so that we can be sure we have covered all eventualities?*

Stick strictly to facts and evidence, your Blue customer is not interested in your personal opinion. To enable them to make a decision, they need plenty of background information, demonstrable evidence and practical studies. They want to be absolutely sure that they will not make a mistake with this decision. You can support them in this by explaining logically why this or that solution is tailor-made for their problem. Show them the advantages and disadvantages, and conceal nothing. If they come across conflicting information later, they will think that you deliberately withheld information.

Give the Blue customer time to absorb the information and digest the facts. Do not pressurise them to give you a quick answer. Allow them time to think.

Be persistent and do not give up when you encounter scepticism. Keep on asking where exactly their doubts lie and explaining the features and benefits patiently and precisely.

As far as written material is concerned, you can furnish them with data, quotations, instructions for use, technical descriptions and business reports beforehand as a preparation for your personal presentation. To use the example of a car showroom again: A Blue motorist typically keeps a log-book, calculates the fuel consumption and draws up a cost-investment analysis to find out whether a car meets their expectations. Car salespeople confirm that it is very reassuring for Blue customers if they give them this information beforehand. The more test results a Blue customer has before them, the easier it is for them to make a decision.

The focus of your presentation and the material you provide should always be on how the product works. Blues want to be in a position to judge whether you and your product/services represent the best solution for their needs. If possible, demonstrate the application of the product. For example:

I like the way you set about looking for a new washing machine, Ms. Jones. You are very thorough and I admire your concern for the environment. This model is the most efficient on the market in a number of areas that are listed here. At the same time, it is one of our tried and tested, best-selling models. Shall I show you how the energy-saving mode works?

Or, if possible, arrange for the Blue customer to visit one of your customers who already uses the system. Work slowly and carefully towards a specific solution for the customer. Look at every question from all sides. Show them that the solution is the best for them, both in the short and in the long term. This will establish your credibility in their eyes and slowly build up their faith in your competence.

Handling time

Time is a precious commodity for the Blue customer. Like the Red customer, they want to make use of their time as effectively as possible. But for them, this does not mean that everything has to be done as quickly as possible. It means that they will use their time to gather information and not waste it chatting. That is why sales negotiations probably take longest of all with a Blue customer and are most exhausting for you, because they will stretch you to your limits.

They expect you to be absolutely punctual and will always turn up on time themselves for meetings. Meetings will proceed at a slow and leisurely pace, and you must adapt to this pace. Your Blue customer needs time to familiarise themselves with all the details. The Blue's calm facade conceals a lively mind; even though they may seem unmoved, their mind is occupied with a host of possible scenarios and trains of thought.

Choice of words

To adapt to the Blue customer's leisurely pace, you should be careful to speak slowly and thoughtfully. Express yourself precisely and directly and don't repeat everything. Throw in occasional questions to lure the Blue customer out of their shell and in order to find out what they are thinking. Ask practical questions to encourage them to tell you where they have misgivings. But never forget that they will only be willing to voice their doubts if they regard you as competent.

Use expressions such as "well-established", "facts", "The data shows ...", "no risk", "Take your time ...", "'Think about it", "analyse", "back-up information".

Statements to motivate a Blue customer

- A programme like this needs benchmarks that ensure high quality standards. It will satisfy your high-level requirements.
- It's such an important decision, we ought to plan several meetings so that we can be sure to sound out all possibilities.
- I wouldn't be at all surprised if this system was still running long after you have retired and taken up fishing – even though those days are still a long way off.
- Others using this product are very happy with it, and you would probably be able to put it to more effective use than most.
- Why don't you test the system for a while before you make your final decision?
- The experts spent a long time working on this idea until they had developed a high-quality programme.
- Many interesting and very comprehensive studies have been made of this product. The details are all in this dossier. I'll leave it here for you to study.
- Read through all the information at your leisure and draw your own conclusions.

Body language

If you normally tend to make sweeping gestures, try to scale them down for the Blue customer. Instead, use slow, measured gestures that express respectability and thoughtfulness. Keep your distance and maintain a formal stance. Never try to touch the Blue customer or cast glances that require them to express their approval or recognition. The Blue would feel forced into accepting more intimacy than they are prepared to accept. Look them straight in the eye and show them in this way that you stand by everything you say. Your tone of voice should also be calm, controlled, and thoughtful. Maintain the same tone of voice most of the time, with little modulation, and speak in a clear, firm voice.

Closing the deal

It often takes the Blue customer a long time to make up their mind. They will put off making their decision until they have read, analysed and researched all the information available in order to minimise the risk of making a mistake. However, you can offer them incentives to make it easier for them to make up their mind. For example:

> *I think you have all the information, now, Mr Smith. I would just like to add that we have a free hotline and a 24-hour repair service for this special model.*

Draw up a plan of action with fixed appointments and milestones. Make an offer in writing, including all the details you have negotiated. Approach the minor details first and work slowly towards the most important points. Make concrete statements and offers and always honour these.

Confirm everything in writing. Don't pressurise them to close the deal on your very first visit. They need to think everything over in peace, and you should respect this. However, you can emphasise the possible drawbacks, the practical or financial disadvantages of delaying the decision.

Follow-up

The Blue customer is not particularly interested in regular contact. What does interest them, however, is fresh information. So, if you have new products, solutions or developments, or if you can provide informative material or studies on a product you have sold them, send it to them. The Blue customer is always interested in an exchange of practical information.

After all we have said so far, it should go without saying that it is very important to the Blue customer that you are absolutely punctual and honour all agreements you make with them to the letter. And you should be just as exact, practical and determined in your handling of any complaints. It annoys them more than other customers when things do not go as planned, so take care of any problems quickly and efficiently. Offer them incentives that will appease them.

How not to do it

It won't take you long to frighten off a Blue customer if you talk about yourself too much or present your information in a disorganised manner. They won't be able to take you seriously.

Other things which won't impress are: A manner that is too casual or informal, vague statements, superficial comments, failure to answer their questions, pressure, or failure to honour agreements. The Blue customer has high expectations, demands high standards of information and expertise. If you present them with references that turn out to be unreliable or quote someone else's opinion as "evidence", they won't be impressed either.

You can also irritate them if you do not keep your distance: either physically or by making personal remarks or expressing criticism. They will be horrified if you try to manipulate them by offering them bait or telling them a sob story.

CHECKLIST:
STRATEGIES FOR NEGOTIATING WITH
BLUE CUSTOMERS

Establishing trust:
Let your competence and reliability convince them.
Keep your distance.
Don't waste time on personal chat and small talk.

Requirement analysis:
Don't rush them.
Find out exactly what they want.

Information:
Prepare your presentation thoroughly.
Come straight to the point and offer plenty of facts and figures.
Offer written material.
Make sure that all their questions are answered.

Closing the deal:
Let them take their time.
Point all out all the possible disadvantages of delay.
Offer them incentives for a speedy decision.

YOUR CUSTOMER IS A

CO-ORDINATOR

Your customer is definitely Blue, but they still seem to be open and you can sense their personal regard for you? They are probably a Co-ordinator. In contrast to the Co-ordinator described in the last chapter, however, their Blue aspects are more dominant than their Green ones. Nevertheless, you can adapt your strategy to address their "Green factor" specifically, with positive results.

Stress all aspects that promise security

When you are presenting your detailed
product information, lay particular emphasis
on the advantages of your product that
promise them, their colleagues or their
company increased security. Stress your
company's long years of experience in the
field, perhaps even your own experience as a
salesperson if that's appropriate. Offer them
special guarantees if they decide to buy.

Be more personal

Be aware of this customer's cautious personal signals, whether
they are letting you feel their regard for you – though they may
do this in a roundabout way – or whether they admit that they
have doubts about a particular aspect of the deal. They express
emotions in a way a pure Blue never would. Take it seriously and
deal with it, but not by trying to calm them or telling them of your
fears and joys – that would be going too far. Give them practical
information that will help dispel their doubts. For example:

> *I can understand that you are worried that our frozen
> products might not keep long enough. Many of our
> customers voice doubts about this. But so far, they have all
> come to realise that our system offers the optimum period of
> storage. In the unlikely event of any products perishing
> before the storage date stipulated, you can return the
> product to us and we will replace it within three days. If you
> still have misgivings, I will personally see to it that a
> replacement is provided within two days in your case. You
> can rest assured that we would not offer you such a
> guarantee if we were not absolutely convinced of the
> superiority of our system.*

YOUR CUSTOMER IS AN
IMPLEMENTOR

Does your customer demand detailed
information although it is perfectly
clear that they know exactly what they
want? Then they are an Implementor,
but one whose Blue aspects clearly
dominate their Red ones. In this case,
you can include a few elements in your
"Blue strategy" to address specifically
the Red side of their character.

Show them that they are important

As a Blue, they are interested in hearing how others have got on
with your product. As a "part-Red", they are particularly
interested in learning what people they respect and people in high
places think of it. Provide corresponding references. They will be
flattered and convinced. It will show them that you have assessed
their importance correctly and they will take it as proof of your
respect for them. Whenever appropriate, let them know that you
are aware of and admire their achievements. For example:

> *Mr Harris, you have many years of experience with such
> systems and are probably the customer who is most qualified
> to judge the quality of our components. I would be very
> interested to hear what you think.*

Offer the highest quality

This example illustrates another aspect that is very important to
the Implementor. They are not only concerned with details and a
safe, tried and tested solution. To a greater extent than the pure
Blue customer, they appreciate high-quality products. Offer them
the best you have, and present it as the best. Take their ideas into

consideration and try to find a solution together with your customer, a solution that is creative, pragmatic and first-class. See it as a personal challenge for yourself, because the Implementor will probably teach you something about your own product. They will appreciate your commitment to solving their problems and your competence in seeking a solution.

HOW DO YOU SELL TO A BLUE CUSTOMER IF YOU YOURSELF ARE ...

... a Blue salesperson?
- You won't have any problems, because you are just as keen on details as they are. The only thing you have to beware of is that you do not get bogged down in the exchange of information and thus never get around to closing the deal.

... a Red salesperson?
- Present plenty of evidence and facts.
- Answer their questions patiently.
- Don't rush them.
- Show them respect.

... a Yellow salesperson (opposite type)?
- Don't tell them stories or reveal personal information.
- Prepare more thoroughly than for other customers.
- Don't express your feelings.

... a Green salesperson?
- Don't let their frequent questions and scepticism unsettle you.

ARE YOU A BLUE SALESPERSON?

Here is a summary of important strategies you can employ with the four colour styles, if you are a Blue salesperson:

Customer's colour style	Red	Yellow	Green	Blue
Opening	Get straight down to business	Be sociable, even if it hurts Talk about the customer	Be direct, open and show a personal interest	Come straight to the point
Asking questions	Concentrate on their goals and how they can be achieved	Don't get bogged down in details	Show interest Talk about personal opinions	Do not be distracted by irrelevant details
Presentation	Focus on the advantages for them and for their goals	Stress future advantages and suggest solutions by means of anecdotes	Involve them Show your human side	Logical and methodical, natural
Confirmation	Show them options with a high likelihood of success	Offer incentives and special terms	Give personal assurances	Don't push them Offer written material
Follow-up	Confirm the proposals and concentrate on the end result	Be clear and direct Concentrate on the future	Give assurances and get in touch regularly	Make a record of the details – how and why
General	Offer them options and proceed at his pace	Show an interest in them	Be sincere, not threatening	Accept the less than perfect

14:

WHEN CUSTOMERS ARE UNDER STRESS: HOW TO REACT

You can never prepare for all eventualities – there will always be surprises. Even your best customer may greet you brusquely one day and angrily sweep your price list from the desk. They may be under stress and suddenly react in a way you have never seen them react before. I am sure you can think of several situations where customers of yours have been under stress and you no longer knew how to calm them down.

Each of the four colour styles reacts in a different way under stress. The examples below will show you how to deal with stress in each style. What are the triggers? How can you learn to recognise the signals of stress in your customers? How do you deal with stressful situations.

THE RED CUSTOMER

Kevin Brash is rather surly this morning. You are already familiar with his rather brusque manner from earlier visits, but this morning he is downright unfriendly. He barks into the intercom for his assistant to appear on the double. When his secretary informs him that his assistant has not arrived yet and that she hasn't heard from him, he completely loses his cool. With a bright red face and an accusing manner – as if it were all your fault! – he informs you curtly that it is his assistant who has done the preparation for your meeting.

> *That's what happens when I don't do everything myself. You had to make an appointment first thing in the morning, didn't you? I always see salespeople in the afternoons. You can't rely on anyone. Now we have to sit around and wait. I've got better things to do with my time. I can't wait all day.*

He goes on and on in this vein, letting you know that he agreed to this morning appointment just to please you and contrary to his usual habits. The minutes that pass before his assistant arrives seem like hours, and you feel really sorry for the poor man. After a real dressing-down and under the angry eyes of his boss, he has to try to concentrate on presenting his company's requirements. You are already doubtful if anything can ever come of these negotiations. If it was up to you, you would prefer to give up and leave right now.

Analysis

What is triggering the stress? Kevin is losing control of things. He had made a concession to you (an early appointment) and now it's gone wrong. He feels helpless because he cannot do anything about the situation. He has no clear target for his meeting with you and he is dependent on a subordinate – a terrible feeling for a Red. He is undecided, doesn't know what to do: You are the witness to a lack of good management on his part, as one of his employees is not honouring agreements. He sees this as a sign of disrespect. He is forced to wait, something he hates.

What are the signals? The early appointment was already a source of annoyance to Kevin, as his unfriendly manner revealed. He is already seething and only needs a spark to set off an explosion. And when he blows his top, he doesn't do things by halves: He becomes aggressive, speaks loudly or shouts. He exaggerates. He makes no secret of his impatience. He is not at all worried about his assistant (after all, he might have had an accident), but sees his failure to arrive punctually as a sign of incompetence. Instead of looking for a solution, he stubbornly clings to his anger, even though he knows that it is not productive. He treats you unfairly. After all, it's not your fault that he agreed to an early morning appointment. You didn't know he was acting against his better judgement.

What can you do? Whatever you do, don't let him intimidate you. And don't feel you have to defend yourself. Neither should you get into a discussion about who is to blame. If his tirades get too much, try to divert him with a question: "Kevin, what could we do to maximise the value of the time we have?". It is important to steer him back into a situation where he can take action, be in control, so that he does not work himself up into even more of a rage. If possible, get him talking about an aspect of your relationship that you have been meaning to talk to him about for a long time. But it must be a subject that really interests him. Alternatively, offer to postpone the meeting. And remember never to make an early morning appointment with him again!

Stress situation – Red customer

Triggers	His authority is undermined
	Tasks he has assigned have been carried out incompetently
	Waste of his time, waiting
	Dependence on others
	He has no clear goal
	Indecisiveness in himself and others.
Stress signals	Shouting, reprimands
	Exaggerated description of the situation and its consequences
	Blames others, is unfair
	Actions are moody and abrupt

Intervention	Suggest neutral subjects in connection with work to fill in the time profitably
	Put him in a situation where he can act and make decisions
	Make good use of the time
	Point out advantages, profit, or benefit
	Ignore accusations or, in a friendly tone, refuse to accept them; refuse to defend yourself
	Stay friendly, accept no responsibility for things that are not your fault
	Offer to postpone the appointment.

THE YELLOW CUSTOMER

You have an appointment to see Joey Flex. You have always spoken to his colleague before, but Joey took over this area of responsibility a few weeks ago. He is very open-minded and easygoing, and you get on well with him. Today, in the course of your conversation, you mention an agreement you made with his colleague. Joey obviously doesn't know about this agreement and is angry. He phones his colleague, but puts down the phone after a short while, in an even worse mood than before. You notice that he is getting more and more nervous. He is distracted, digs around in the piles of papers on his desk, ostensibly looking for something, tells you by the way that he had lunch with his colleague in the canteen only last week. He really could have told him about the agreement! Then he starts to explain in great detail why the food they serve in the canteen is terrible. Gradually, you learn that Joey had a completely different idea of this deal and that his hands are now tied because of the agreement his colleague made with you:

Everything has to go according to the book here. Everyone sees just their own little concerns and no one passes on information. Why did he make an agreement with you when he knew he was due to hand the business over to me?

These and other statements clearly display his anger, and he lets you know that you are partly to blame, too. After all, you also knew that his colleague would be handing over to him. Then he explains to you in great detail how much better his idea is and why, but it's all decided already, anyway. In the end, it's clear that nothing is going to come of the meeting, because Joey is clearly not capable of coming up with a new solution. He is too busy moaning about his colleague and you in particular and his fate in general.

Analysis

What is triggering the stress? Joey has realised that others know more than he does about something that is his concern. He doesn't like that one bit. His colleague has withheld information from him and now he has had to rely on you to tell him what is going on. He feels left out, something it seems has happened before in his dealings with that particular colleague and in this company. He feels fenced in, cannot be as flexible as he would like to be, cannot exercise his creativity. He had a completely different idea of things, and now he has found out that the whole matter has already been decided on. No one is interested in his idea, and that hurts.

What are the signals? He talks and talks, but comes no closer to a solution for the real problem. He behaves in a manner exactly contrary to that which is normal for him – he becomes inflexible, more and more confused. He talks about trivia (food in the canteen). He gets involved in a long and pointless debate in which he appears self-opinionated and argumentative. He argues with everything you say, even though his standpoint is illogical. And if you prove him wrong on one point, he will move on to the next.

What can you do? As soon as you can, interrupt the conversation in a friendly manner, chat for a while about something or other and make a new appointment to meet. It is important to interrupt your meeting if you have reached stalemate. Go for a coffee or take a break. Or you can try to find a compromise, to negotiate a new deal with Joey. It could be a long process, though!

Stress situation – Yellow customer

Trigger	He has been left out
	Something is going on behind his back
	Others are not being open with him
	His ideas are not being taken seriously
	His flexibility is curbed
	Criticism of his volatility.
Stress signals	Becomes argumentative, self-opinionated, over-critical
	Becomes inflexible, insists on unimportant details
	Talks non-stop, jumps from one topic to the next.
Intervention	Take a break
	Activate his creativity
	Praise him, give reassurance
	Put the situation in its right perspective
	Always return to the subject in hand, but remain friendly
	Express understanding.

THE GREEN CUSTOMER

You have arranged to meet your customer, John Becker. Instead, his colleague, Susan Friendly, is waiting for you. She was present at your last meeting with John, but she was so quiet that you didn't really register her presence. She explains that John is ill and that she will be conducting the meeting in his place. This is no problem for you, you only wonder why Susan is so stiff and formal. Perhaps that's just her manner. You have reached a point in your negotiations with John where you could expect a few decisions to be made on the nature and range of the order they will be placing. As Susan is no stranger to you, you get down to business fairly soon, but notice that Susan immediately clams up. Unfortunately, you also have to explain to her that the delivery period has altered. You are no longer able to deliver by the deadline you spoke of last time they met. Susan is horrified: She cannot accept that you are suddenly going back on your word. She asks again and again if there is not some way to keep to the delivery date you had planned. It seems as if she might let the whole deal fall through because of it. She does not react to any of your other points or make any other decisions. She has to talk to John Becker first. This is annoying for you. You might as well not have come.

Analysis

What is triggering the stress? Susan feels that you completely neglected her at your last meeting. You did not involve her in the conversation and made no attempt to talk to her. She expected more of you. After all, she is a customer, too. She is personally insulted by your impersonal manner. She also feels insecure because she cannot work out why you do not "like" her. Then, to top it all, you confront her with a sudden change of plan, which completely throws her off-balance. She has to make decisions she was not expecting – so she feels even more insecure.

What are the stress signals? The first sign of pending misunderstanding was Susan's reserve. You did not meet her need for an atmosphere of trust, so she withdrew, insulted. And when she was then also confronted with the change in delivery date, she fought vehemently against the alteration in her plans. She takes up a position that is the contrary of her normal manner: She fights like a lioness and refuses to accommodate you in any way. She cannot admit that flexibility is now required. She fixes all her attention on questions of procedure and is determined to find a way to make the impossible happen.

What can you do? You can make good what you did wrong in your last meeting. First, bring the conversation onto a personal level and show her that you hold her in high regard. Ask her about her work and her ideas. Involve her. Only return to the subject of the deal when you can see that she has now forgiven you and is prepared to do business with you. Explain to her exactly why there is a delay in delivery and ask for her understanding. Allow her enough time to get used to the change in plan.

Stress situation – Green Customer

Trigger	Impersonal manner of business partners No atmosphere of trust Sudden changes of plan Quick decisions.
Stress signals	Extreme caution and reserve Avoids taking risks and making decisions Tries to shift the decision to someone else Digs their heels in Tries to maintain the *status quo* In extreme cases, complete withdrawal and refusal to co-operate further.
Intervention	Make assurances of your personal regard Shift to the required level for the relationship Reduce the problem to more manageable dimensions Answer all questions Allow plenty of time.

THE BLUE CUSTOMER

You have made an appointment to meet two customers in a company. When you arrive, you discover that one of them is ill. Noel Clear will be conducting the meeting alone. You notice that he is not only more reserved than usual, but really tense. He hardly looks at you, but stares at his list, on which he has made a note of the points that you are to discuss today. You are surprised. Up to now, you have seen him as a quiet but competent person in command of the situation. He fires off his first question almost before you have sat down. However, instead of answering, you say:

> I'm sorry, Mr. Clear, but we cannot install your XYZ software until a month later than planned. I'm terribly sorry, but our technicians are fully booked until then. I would suggest the 15th May, and I would appreciate it if you could tell me today whether this date is convenient for you.

Noel Clear freezes. What's this? His colleague is the one who knows all about this programme. He can only find three pages of information on it. He starts asking questions. He wants to know everything, right down to the finest details. You can feel yourself becoming impatient. You have already discussed these details at great length. You indicate subtly that you feel it is not necessary to go into such detail again. But he won't give up. He starts to draw up a flow chart to prove that this installation date is not possible. That gets on your nerves. His problems are really peanuts compared to what's going on in your own company. Noel makes long pauses, stares into thin air and is obviously not in a position to think clearly, let alone make a decision.

Analysis

What is triggering the stress? Noel Clear found himself in an unusual situation and with more responsibility than he is accustomed to bearing. That made him insecure from the outset.

Then he is also confronted with an unexpected change of plan that requires him to make an immediate decision. That is something he cannot handle. In his mind, he is painting worst-case scenarios, can already see himself losing his job because he made the wrong decision. That's why he needs information. The more information he has, the clearer he will see what he should do, is his reasoning. But he never has enough information. There is always some important detail missing. At the same time, it is very embarrassing for him to sit there like a fool, not in control and unable to express his opinion competently, as he usually does. He is so caught up in his own worries that the simplest solution, namely to pick up the phone and ask his colleague what he thinks, doesn't even cross his mind.

What are the stress signals? Withdrawal and tension are the signals of stress in a Blue, which are often overlooked because he is such a quiet person. Because he normally likes to ask a lot of questions, his questions in stress situations are only latent signals. It only becomes obvious that he is under stress when he no longer absorbs your answers to his questions. He falls into completely atypical behavioural patterns, becomes nervous and chaotic, roots around in the papers on his desk and asks a multitude of illogical and unstructured questions. He becomes over-precise, weighs everything up, searches meticulously for the logic in everything, goes over the pros and cons again and again in his mind. He withdraws into himself, which may lead to his worst fears coming true. He seems unapproachable or becomes angry.

What can you do? First and foremost, you can satisfy his need for information. If you become impatient, you will not be respecting his needs. The thing a Blue under stress needs most is time. You should also provide as much feedback and emotional support as possible: "I can understand that the situation takes you by surprise. Let's go through it together. I'm sure you will make the right decision if we take a look at the situation carefully".

Stress situation – Blue customer

Trigger	Too much responsibility
	Unexpected change of plan
	Pressure of time
	Quick decision required
	Fears they have not enough information.
Stress signals	Withdrawal
	Many questions, but unstructured
	Disjointed movements, nervousness
	Annoyance, accusations
	Tries to shirk responsibility.
Intervention	Allow him time
	Answer questions calmly
	Confirm his competence
	Slow down
	Provide structure
	Provide detailed information.

CONCLUSION

The natural reaction to one of your customers in a stressful situation is the further expression of their dominant control – Greens avoid conflict, Blues withdraw, Yellows get boisterous and Reds more aggressive. So learn to become a "stress-reader" in these situations to get a successful outcome. Next time one of your customers is under stress in a sales meeting, try these strategies to see what works best. However, don't be surprised if you don't manage to defuse the situation first time around.

Think of yourself first. If you let your customer's stress become your own, you have already lost. If you stay calm, observe the situation closely, and only then intervene carefully, you have won. The more often you master such situations, the easier it will become to deal with stressful situations in the future, and your customers will appreciate the fact that you do not become impatient or take it personally, but behave in a manner which shows your understanding of **their** situation.

15:
How to Handle "Natural" Objections

The first thing your customer says is: "I'm not buying anything! I just need some information! I don't need your products!" Don't let that deter you. This could be your best ever customer! In reality, that's all just a threatening gesture: The truth is that this is a customer who can't say "No".

Not every customer will enthusiastically shake your hand to seal the deal as soon as you have presented your product to them – unfortunately! Some customers will reject you from the first, and you won't always be able to explain why. "Resistance" is a fact of life in the selling profession. Your customer may be having problems with their own sales figures. They may have had a bad experience with your predecessor, or they want to prove to their boss that they are not someone a salesperson can lead up the garden path. Perhaps they enjoy exercising their "power" as a potential buyer and are hoping that these tactics will give them an advantage over you when you get down to discussing price.

There are many reasons why a customer might treat you coolly, and most of them have nothing to do with you as a person. The first step in dealing with a "wilful" customer is not to take anything on an emotional level and not to react to their defensiveness by being on the defensive yourself. Concentrate on recognising these signals and reacting calmly. You can "save" many situations just by keeping your cool and intervening with small gestures. This is sure to earn you your customers' respect.

EXERCISE:
WHEN WAS THE LAST TIME YOU
"CAME UP AGAINST A BRICK WALL"?

Remember the last meeting where you had the feeling your customer was being obstructive, when they contradicted everything you said and you just could not get through to them.

What exactly did your customer say to "send you packing"?
Describe their manner.
Describe their facial expression.
What were your feelings?
Could you understand why they were reacting in this way?
Was there something in the way you acted that might have caused their reaction?

Be careful with self-criticism. When others are in a bad mood, it is seldom your fault. Nevertheless, consider the possibility that it might be something you said or did. You know so much about the colour styles now that you will certainly not react to this on a personal level. It could be that your customer is a "Red" type, and that you yourself as a "Green" just make him "see red"! If you can see things on this level, you can approach the problem logically and consider appropriate strategies.

CONFRONTATION AND CURTNESS –
THE RED CUSTOMER'S WAY OF
SHOWING THEIR REJECTION

Message: "I am not going to let you get through to me."
- *They lure you into a trap or make you feel awkward:* The Red customer tries to shake you by saying quite openly: "You're

talking rubbish!" or "You don't seriously expect me to believe that, do you?"
- *They quite clearly demonstrate their rejection of you:* They categorically deny everything you say: "That's ridiculous!" or "Rubbish!"
- *They continually make negative comments:* They keep throwing in negative and disparaging remarks like: "There's no way that's going to work", "That's illogical" or "That can't be true"
- *They are deliberately rude:* They yawn openly or demonstrate their impatience in some other way.
- *They keep interrupting you:* Before you can finish a sentence, the customer interrupts. They are always just a step ahead of you and finish your sentences for you.
- *They become sarcastic:* They make spiteful or sneering remarks such as: "You think you're a real expert, don't you?" or "You've got that off pat, haven't you?"
- *They become argumentative:* They become aggressive or insulting.
- *They become contemptuous:* They try to put you down by claiming to understand more about the matter than you do.

Your counter-strategy
- Ask polite counter-questions: "What is it you don't understand?" or "Why don't you feel able to believe me?"
- Be self-confident and don't let them intimidate you. That is the best way to earn their respect.
- Remain objective and ignore their rudeness.
- Ask them how they see things. Allow them to take action and get them back to the business in hand. Allow them to make a decision.
- If they will not stop: Ask them to concentrate on the business in hand: "Let's keep to the subject."
- Or confront them: "Please explain exactly what it is that is bothering you. Then we can do something about it."

Ignoring You Politely – Yellow Customers Smile and Chat

Message: "I don't want your product, but I don't want an argument either."

- *They hide behind a mask of politeness:* They listen to you, seemingly polite and attentive, but their thoughts are somewhere else completely and they are not really absorbing what you are saying. You are taken in by their enthusiasm and then get a shock when they do not buy.
- *They agree with everything you say:* They nod, agree, are enthusiastic, say "Great" or "Wonderful". But they are exaggerating. Their comments don't really fit what you are saying at that moment and you can tell that they do not mean them.
- *They wander off the subject:* They jump from one subject to another and only touch on each superficially.
- *They ask "easy" questions:* They avoid subjects that are unpleasant or complicated. If a difficult point crops up, they blame themselves and apologise for mentioning it. When you sense an objection there and want to talk about it, they vehemently deny having a problem with it at all.
- *Their manner is overly sociable:* They are reluctant to get down to business and waste time making harmless small talk.

Your counter-strategy
- Remain friendly, but always come back to the business in hand.
- Make a concrete offer and set a deadline for them to accept or refuse it. Come back to this point again and again.
- Ask them straight out whether they are interested.
- Try to awaken their interest by telling them about other customers whom they may know.
- Arouse their creative urge. Try spinning ideas with them for a while, always seeing them in relation to the concrete situation.

- Give them a friendly smile and ask them with slight irony: "You don't really want to buy, am I right?". Often, disarming honesty will get you an honest answer. If they return your smile and confirm your suspicions, leave it be. You will have won them as a customer for another project.

RESERVE AND RESTLESSNESS – GREEN CUSTOMERS ARE NERVOUS

Message: "Keep your distance!"
- *They are silent:* They do not react, their face is expressionless. You can see no sign that your message is getting through.
- *They become restless and fidgety:* They fidget around on their seat, shift their weight from one foot to the other, drum on the table with their fingertips, and look around the room.
- *They answer mechanically:* They give you short, non-committal answers: "I don't know" or "Hard to say"
- *They show signs of apathy:* They seem bored, indifferent, disinterested and appear to want to get the presentation over as soon as possible.

Your counter-strategy
- Go back to the phase of establishing trust. Perhaps you have been proceeding too quickly.
- Ask them concrete questions to make them give up their passive role.
- Ask them what further information they require. Signal that you have the time to answer any questions.
- Ask them whether they simply need time to think it over. But set a deadline and then contact them.
- If possible, show them what advantages your product would have for themselves and their family.

Rigid Masks and Resistance – Blue Customers Ask Questions until You Go of Your Own Accord

Message: "Just don't talk me into buying inferior products."

- *They are "unmoved"*: They try not to show any physical reactions. Neither their eyes nor facial expression reveal anything about their thoughts or feelings. If they move at all, it's only backwards: Their upper body leans backwards or they take a step backwards in order to put a greater distance between themselves and the salesperson.
- *Their answer are monotone*: They do not ask any more questions, and only answers your questions briefly. They look at their watch and explain that they have run out of time. They are no longer prepared to devote to this meeting with you any more of the time that they otherwise devote to the search for interesting information.
- *They are looking at alternative offers*: They won't be nailed down, are fussy or draw open comparisons with other offers. They show you openly that they have solicited offers from your competitors (or that they intend to do so) and that they expect more favourable offers there.
- *They demand more and more information from you*: They reject every point you make in your presentation, but this is often a way of getting more information from you or testing you to find out whether you are really competent. It can also be a pretext to avoid making a decision.

Your counter-strategy

- Take your time, give them the information they need.
- Interrupt the meeting. Send them plenty of written material and make a new appointment with them.
- Show them that you are an expert. Be self-assured, but whatever you don't do, don't pressurise them.

- Ask them what your offer lacks in their eyes. Show them that you are interested in their needs.
- Keep to the business in hand and do not try to divert them or "loosen them up" by throwing in a few personal anecdotes: They won't wash with them.

The most important thing in difficult situations is to remain calm and collected: To be neither superior nor arrogant, nor too openly sympathetic. Your customers will appreciate that most.

CONCLUSION

Today, raising objections is second nature to buyers. Objections are really questions for more information and give you a clear indication of where your customer stands in the sales negotiation.

Objections are rarely personal rejections. However, as you have seen, each colour style delivers objections in their own unique way. And each colour style interprets objections from their own perspective.

16:

SELLING OVER THE TELEPHONE

How often do you reach for the phone to acquire a new customer? Is it part of your daily routine or do you avoid telephoning potential new customers wherever possible?

Do you simply pick up the phone and call your (potential) new customer or do you prepare thoroughly? When you are aware of the best way to proceed, the more relaxed you will be subsequently on the phone, and the more convincing you will be!

WHY ARE YOU PHONING A (POTENTIAL) CUSTOMER?

Unless you really need to clarify a point in an ongoing sales process, there are three reasons for telephoning a (potential) customer:

- Acquisition: You would like to win a new customer and make an appointment to visit them.
- Inquiry concerning requirements: You phone one of your customers to find out whether they need anything.
- Looking after customers: You phone one of your customers to keep in touch and reaffirm your relationship.

Phoning strangers for the purpose of acquiring new customers is particularly challenging for young salespeople with little experience. Fear of rejection and failure makes many of them reluctant to phone a complete stranger who probably doesn't need any of their products at that moment anyway.

The more experienced you are, the less often you will have to phone new customers, as you will already have established a network of contacts. This means that it is at the beginning of your career that you have to face this difficult task, one for which you may lack the courage and the self-confidence. But it also means that your prestige and your success are all the greater if you succeed in winning a new customer over the phone!

Try these techniques:

- Collect as much information about the potential customer as you can before you make the phone call. Make inquiries about their position, their areas of responsibility and how they operate. Then you will have a fair idea of what colour style to expect although, of course, it's better to keep an open mind.
- Make as positive an impression as you can. On the phone, as much as 85% of the impact you make is determined by the tone of your voice and only 15% by what you actually say. You will be most convincing if you talk in your own natural, personal style. Aim to sound trustworthy, friendly and professional and not nervous, over-friendly, exaggerated or as if you were reading from a sheet. Practise: Read out loud and notice how much better your voice sounds when you are calm and relaxed. Aim for this tone of voice when conducting sales calls, but without making it sound artificial.
- Speak fluently and smoothly. Don't chop off the end of your sentences, speak slowly but continuously. Speak clearly and loudly. If you mumble, speak too quietly, swallow the ends of sentences or say "eh ..." too often, the person on the other end of the line is going to get bored and it will be too strenuous to listen to you. Smile when you say something pleasant. You can "hear" a smile over the phone.
- Are you proud of your product? Are you convinced of its value? Then let this enthusiasm come over in your voice, but

don't exaggerate here, especially when you are speaking to Blue or Red customers.

- Think of something positive just before you make the call. Think of a past success, the last phone call where you convinced a customer of your product. Imagine your customer as a pleasant person to know in private, setting out on a weekend trip with their family. Imagine that your product is just what your customer has been waiting for and that they will be glad you phoned.

- Your potential new partner is likely to be far more attentive if they develop a high level of respect for you. They will also be more attentive if you speak in a lively and convincing tone. And they will be attentive if what you say concerns them personally, not just on a general level. You must leave a positive impression with your prospect – they must believe that the appointment you make will be of advantage to them. They must be confident of your professionalism, your competence, your reputation in the sector and your experience.

- Be an attentive listener yourself! It's the only way to find out whether your message is getting through and to combat doubts. Listen not just to the customer's words, but more to their tone of voice. If their words and tone are at odds, go by the tone of voice and ask questions to find out the truth.

GENUINE AND FAKED OBJECTIONS

A customer's first reaction over the phone is often negative and cold. Even if they are basically open-minded about your product, often at first they will say "No" on the phone. The best thing you can do is to ignore their rejection. Don't let it discourage you. Question the reasons behind it.

Faked objections are purely defensive mechanisms based on the urge to protect oneself, and starting to discuss these with a customer only leads to a dead end. Faked objections are general excuses that are either obviously illogical or cannot be defended logically if you inquire deeper. The common objections are: "No time", "Not interested", or "We've already got one".

Genuine objections, on the other hand, have a concrete background: If the customer already has such a product, for example, then they can describe it in detail. Then they may discover that you actually have a superior product or service to offer them, and they may be interested in buying from you next time. If you want to make an appointment with this kind of prospect, you must dispel all these genuine objections first. So concentrate on them while you are talking. Your knowledge of the four colour styles will stand you in good stead here. It will help you adapt your method to suit your customer.

Write up a list showing how you can react to genuine objections, or how you can detect faked objections. It will enable you to react more professionally when you hear either kind of objection. But be sure to formulate what you say freely, or it will sound strained. For example:

- *Not interested* – "I can appreciate that you are not interested in something you don't know anything about. But why don't you take a look at the product and judge for yourself. It will only take up a quarter of an hour of your time."
- *Don't need one* – "I can guarantee you two things. First: I will not try to sell you something you do not need. My aim at our first meeting is simply to inform you. Secondly: You will be much better informed than your competitors after our meeting."
- *No time* – "I know you are a very busy person. But that is exactly why you appreciate products that save you time – and my product does just that. The best way for you to judge that is to see it for yourself. I would like to visit you for a demonstration."

How should you address a Red customer on the phone? How to you deal with a Green? Here are tips for all four colour styles.

THE RED CUSTOMER ON THE PHONE

Your voice should radiate self-confidence and professionalism. Whatever you do, don't let your voice reveal that your customer's resistance or their off-hand remarks irritate you.

The right opening

Greet them in a friendly, accommodating, but businesslike tone. Introduce yourself confidently, give your title and briefly introduce your company. The best way to present the advantages of your product is to do so in such a way that it underlines their self-esteem and independence. Then introduce the subject of an appointment.

How will the Red customer react?

You must expect open resistance. Their remarks might be negative, curt, defensive, and they will present them as soon as you pause. They may also answer with a quick "Yes" or a defensive "No". Perhaps they won't even listen to you properly because they already have a preconceived opinion of your product.

How to react to "faked" objections

Allow them to express their negative feelings and do not react. Listen closely. Perhaps you will be able to hear the real reason for their resistance and can respond to it professionally. Ask open questions to find out.

How to react to "genuine" resistance

You should continue to ask questions until you know exactly what bothers them or prevents them showing an interest in your product. Respond to their objections with thoughtful comments. Respect their desire to waste as little time as possible and to achieve quick results. Promise them an efficient and competent presentation. However, you should not expect open agreement, even if they make an appointment with you.

For example, you have made inquiries about the boss of a medium-sized company and have decided that he is probably a Red type.

Salesperson:	Good morning, Mr. Hawkins. My name is Margaret Miller. I am the sales manager of the AnyFinance company. We are investment consultants for an exclusive circle of private customers. At the moment, we are offering new bonds to a small group of new customers, an investment with first-class conditions you will not find anywhere else. They promise a high yield with a calculable risk. Can we make an appointment to talk about it?
Customer:	My money is already well-invested. I'm not interested.
Salesperson:	As the head of a medium-sized enterprise, you are well placed to judge whether an investment is profitable or not. Our yield is around five per cent at the moment. Do your other investments offer higher returns?
Customer:	Send me the brochures. I'll take a look at them.
Salesperson:	Actually, as we are offering this investment exclusively to a small group of new customers, I would like to take the opportunity to describe it to you personally. Allow me to outline the advantages in just a few minutes. They will be minutes well spent for you and the investment promises high profits.'
Customer:	OK, fire away.

Remember: The Red customer sometimes buys at once! He doesn't even have to see you face to face.

THE YELLOW CUSTOMER ON THE PHONE

The right opening

Speak in a friendly tone of voice, but don't overdo it. Present your product in a way that emphasises its advantages for others. If necessary, offer a reference from a mutual acquaintance. Mention this acquaintance several times by name. The Yellow customer will be impressed that you know them. However, don't overdo it.

How will the Yellow customer react?

The Yellow customer will probably be quite enthusiastic, if non-committal, and will not ask many questions, but unfortunately, their "workload" or "full schedule" will not allow them to make an appointment to meet you personally. Be prepared for the fact that they will not show any genuine business interest in your product.

However, anything is possible with this customer: Perhaps they really are enthusiastic and will immediately make a firm appointment with you. But perhaps they were not really listening to what you told them and, when you meet them, they won't remember exactly what made them so enthusiastic about your product.

How to react to "faked" objections

A Yellow customer who feels pressurised may start to defend their *status quo*. Give them security.

Ask them closed questions that they can only answer with "Yes" or "No" responses.

How to react to "genuine" objections

Ask as many questions as you need to find out exactly where their objections lie. They may exaggerate the situation a little. You should guide the conversation. Don't let them talk for too long: interrupt them and stick to the subject.

You should not give up until they have agreed to see you. Offer them alternative meeting times: "How does Tuesday at 3.15 pm suit you for an appointment or would you prefer Wednesday at 11.30 am?".

THE GREEN CUSTOMER ON THE PHONE

The right opening

Strike a warm, relaxed note, but above all don't be too "smarmy". State the advantages of your product that offer them, their family or their company increased security.

How will the Green customer react?

A Green prospect may say nothing, and appear disinterested and indifferent. If they are interested in your product, they will inquire cautiously but will avoid making any commitments.

How to react to "faked" objections

If they make excuses or don't say anything, give them time, don't rush them. Ask questions until you know where their doubts really lie. There is no need to react immediately to curt or negative answers. They may not be real signs of doubt – maybe they are hesitant. Of the four colour styles, a Green customer makes it most difficult for you to judge which of their objections are genuine and which are faked, as they are naturally reluctant to express their misgivings. You can make it easier for yourself by repeatedly inquiring into the grounds for their objections and, by a process of elimination, casting aside the faked objections one by one as you discover them.

How to react to "genuine" objections

If the customer has a genuine reason for misgivings, deal with the problem intensively. Show them that you take their doubts seriously and that you are personally interested in the contact with them.

Ask open questions and discuss things with them. Make sure they have a chance to express their opinion, that you don't talk the whole time. Never assume that silence means agreement. You must persuade them to express their approval or disapproval openly. Encourage them to voice their misgivings by showing them that you will not take it personally, that you can handle their doubts. However, don't expect enthusiasm and don't pressurise them into making a quick decision. They may also request written material from you, but be careful that they do not use this as an excuse to postpone things. You may be able to persuade a Green customer to make an appointment with you if you emphasise the advantages of taking the time to discuss things thoroughly person-to-person, face-to-face.

THE BLUE CUSTOMER ON THE PHONE

The right opening

The best thing to do with a Blue customer is to send them plenty of written information beforehand, which you can then refer to when you phone them. Strike a businesslike note, speak slowly and in short sentences, leaving out all unnecessary, meaningless phrases. Try to give what you say a logical structure. When you describe your product, emphasise all the advantages and benefits for their company. A Blue customer does not like you to address them too often by their first name. To them, that is a sign of inappropriate familiarity.

How will the Blue customer react?

If they find the written material you have sent interesting, they will probably ask you straight away about your own background, that of your company and your product. If they are not interested, they may answer with a firm "No". You should also be prepared for long pauses for thought while talking to this customer. However, they do not always mean rejection. Your Blue customer is simply thinking about the next step.

How to react to "faked" objections

The Blue customer uses faked objections as delaying tactics. While they are holding you "at arm's length" with their doubts, they are really thinking about whether it might not be to their advantage to talk to you after all. So it is better to allow them the time to think. Accept pauses, don't become nervous or try to hurry them. You can ask them why they are silent: "Are you thinking about something? What is it?".

How to react to "genuine" objections

Ask open questions to find out more about them. To find out their precise requirements, ask "What?", "How?" and "Why?". Talk to them at length about their misgivings and questions. Allow a real discussion of all the pros and cons. But don't expect immediate agreement when you think they must be convinced by now. If necessary, offer to send them more material, but don't let them fob you off without making an appointment to visit them. Give them time and be persistent. You can expect a Blue customer either to make a firm appointment or to refuse, in which case they will give their reasons for doing so.

IF THE CUSTOMER HAS AGREED TO SEE YOU

Whatever colour your prospect, follow these points to position yourself to maximum advantage:

- Make an exact appointment – date, place and time.
- Show them you are flexible, ask them for example: "Is the 15th convenient for you, or would the 16th be better?", naming the date you would prefer in second place. Customers with strong Red aspects like to have a choice.
- Arrange to meet at an "in-between" time, for example 3.30 rather than 3 o'clock. This makes you seem more competent and well-organised. In the case of Blue and Green customers, you can indicate that you will then be completely at their disposal: "After 5.30, I've got all the time we need to answer all your questions".
- Send them written confirmation of the appointment.
- Don't replace the receiver the minute you have said "Goodbye". Wait until the customer replaces their receiver first. It makes a bad impression if they hear you slam the receiver down immediately, as if you were thinking: "Phew! Thank goodness that's over".

IF THE CUSTOMER HAS REFUSED TO SEE YOU

If all your efforts have been in vain and the customer really does not want to make an appointment with you, at least try to pave the way for an appointment at some time in the future:

- Arrange to phone them again at some time in the future: "I understand that you don't require anything at the moment. But perhaps I could contact you again in six months' time? Your requirements may have changed by then". Or: "From what you've told me, I really think we have the right products for you, but I can see that you don't need them at the moment. When can I phone you again?"

- Address the customer's feelings without placing them under any obligation: "If you were going to buy from us, what sort of service would you expect?" Or: "I would like to see whether you would be satisfied with our service. What do you expect of a supplier?"
- Never give up, phone back after the agreed period. Most of your potential customers will be impressed by your persistence.

17:

SELLING AT TRADE FAIRS

THE RIGHT ATTITUDE

Always enter a trade fair with the right attitude: It's going to be hectic, it's going to be hard work, but it will be worth it. You won't convince anyone if you are unwilling or less than enthusiastic about the potential of a trade fair to promote your products or services.

Trade fairs are also an opportunity to be really creative. You will have opportunities to talk to many people. You can find out far more quickly which colour style a visitor belongs to because they are outside their comfort zone.

Set yourself concrete goals: To speak to X current customers, to make appointments to see Y prospective customers. Goals will make you more ambitious. Even if you don't quite achieve the target you set yourself, you are far more likely to be above the result you would have achieved if you hadn't set a target at all!

INDICATE YOUR WILLINGNESS TO ADVISE

While you are standing on your stand at the fair, remember what we have said about the impression you make: Your body language is the most important communication factor. No matter how carefully you choose your words, if your composure and gestures say something completely different, that is the message (and lasting impression) the customer goes away with.

Some further tips:

- Stand where you will be seen. Don't hang around in corners or on the edges of your display stand. You should sit down only if you really need a rest. When talking to a visitor, you should always be on the same "level". Stand up when someone speaks to you.

- Your body language and your facial expression should tell the visitor that they can approach you, that you will take time to speak to them. Smile in a friendly and interested manner, maintaining eye contact. Turn your body towards someone who wants to speak to you. However, don't overdo it. If you are too enthusiastic, you may frighten off Red or Blue visitors. Be accommodating but professional and businesslike at all times.

- Wear a nameplate. Let people know who you are.

- Don't chat to colleagues when there are visitors (for example, Greens) near you who might want to speak to you but are afraid to interrupt your conversation.

BRIEF CONVERSATIONS

At trade fairs, conversations with potential customers will be briefer than usual, there is a lot more going on around you and there are many people waiting to claim your attention. This makes it particularly difficult to establish trust. You will have to work really hard at it if you want to persuade your customer to have confidence in you in just a brief, ten-minute interview. You don't have much time to tell your customer why it would be worth their while to do business with you, and this means it is all the more important to strike just the right note to suit the customer's style and to "speak their language".

The golden rule is: Be brief. Present your most important points in a relaxed, friendly tone, but strip it right down to the bare essentials. Save the rest for a later appointment. You should be able to introduce your company in just 30 seconds. You can decide before the fair how you are going to do this. Ask your new prospects why they are at the fair and what your company might be able to do for them. It is perfectly in order to be a bit more direct than normal, as your visitor will probably want to visit a few other stands as well. However, if you are aware that you are proceeding a little too fast for them, slow down.

YOUR PRESENTATION AT FAIRS

It is often difficult to concentrate at trade fairs. There are so many things going on to distract your attention: Prospective customers are waiting to speak to you, regular customers expect preferential treatment, loudspeakers are announcing a special event and you have an important appointment in a quarter of an hour. Nevertheless, your visitor expects you to listen to them and devote all your attention to their situation.

After the initial greetings, you should proceed to the analysis of your prospect's/customer's requirements. Ask them specific questions about their company and their products. Listen attentively to their answers and pay attention to their tone of voice, gestures and expression in order to establish as quickly as possible their colour style. Once you know this, you can adapt your presentation to suit their style. Summarise what they have told you so far, and ask whether you have understood correctly. Then present your product briefly and professionally, showing how your customer could benefit from it. Depending on their colour style, you should emphasise the economic, the social or qualitative benefits. Conclude by suggesting that you make an appointment for a later date when you will both have more time and when you can offer more detailed information. For example:

> I'll prepare a few options for you. Then you can make up your mind.

Or:

> *Why don't we make an appointment to talk about it? Then*
> *we can go into all the details. Would next week be*
> *convenient for you?*

Decide whether your discussions at the fair are real sales
negotiations where you can expect to conclude a deal, or whether
your aim should only be to interest a potential new customer in
your products and arrange a further appointment with them.

THE FOUR COLOUR STYLES AS VISITORS AT TRADE FAIRS

The Red at a Trade Fair

Reds expect you to provide them with information, and want you
to do it competently and in a businesslike manner. They want to
get the most out of their visit and to take away as much
information as possible. They know exactly what they want and
will immediately confront you with concrete questions. Answer
these questions just as concretely, don't tell them the whole story.
You can offer them incentives and tips – if they are interested,
they will ask more questions. They will interrupt you and perhaps
tell you about the disadvantages of your product. Ignore these
provocations. If they raise genuine objections, counter them, but
try not to let them involve you in a discussion.

Stress all the advantages and benefits of your product/service
that save the customer time, increase their productivity, tighten
up their organisation, or give them a competitive edge. Emphasise
the results – the added value – and not the way the product
works. Handled carefully, this customer may close the deal with
you right there, on your stand.

The Yellow at a Trade Fair

Yellows are in their element at a trade fair. A trade fair is held to
facilitate contacts, and the Yellow wants to get to know as many

new people as possible. They are out to collect names and business cards, and also to have fun. This means they will not spend much time on your stand (or any other, since they are keen to move on and meet new people).

In their first conversation with you, they are less interested in your product than in you, so tell them something about yourself. If you can fit in a few jokes or witty remarks, they will remember you, and you can refer back to this encounter when you contact them after the fair.

Don't try to do business with a Yellow customer at a trade fair, and don't try to discuss business with them either, unless they insist on it. It's unlikely that much will come of it, and they are unlikely to remember you after the fair. If they ask you about your product, don't tell them all the details. Instead, describe the feeling your product will give them, how it will make their life richer, easier, more interesting or entertaining.

"I just wanted to say 'Hello' " is the motto of your regular customer (Yellow) who visits your stand at the fair. All they require from you is the confirmation of a brief contact, a smile, a pleasantry or perhaps an arrangement to meet for dinner.

The Green at a Trade Fair

Greens will probably approach you very hesitantly, because they are afraid of disturbing you or that you will not have time for them. All the hustle and bustle of the trade fair is probably too much for them, and it will take a lot of encouragement and patience on your part to deal with them. If you take the time to talk to them, they will have positive memories of their visit to your stand.

Greens would prefer to talk to you in private. Try to offer them a relaxed atmosphere in a quiet corner and ask lots of questions if they seem to be a promising customer. Present your company as trustworthy and very experienced. Stress its reliability, the service and the warranty periods. And make a follow-up appointment.

The main thing when you are talking to a Green customer at trade fairs is to establish a basis of trust. You can then discuss the business details at your next appointment.

The Blue at a Trade Fair

Blues only want information, they are not interested in personal contact. They like trade fairs because they enable them to compare the products directly. So they ask for details and then pop off to see whether your competitor's product also has this feature – or *vice versa*. Take the time to give them comprehensive information if they seem a promising customer. Show them that you are an expert so that they will respect you as a future business partner. Be sure to provide them with enough reading matter to take home. Insist on getting their business card – they will probably be reluctant to give it to you. Then you can phone them after the fair and refer to the material you gave them.

You probably won't see many of your regular customers who are Blues at the trade fair, though one might drop in to inform you that your competitors are now offering this or that special feature. You can learn a lot about your competitors' products from a Blue.

18:
BUILD THE IDEAL SALES TEAM

Would you like to be part of a top-performing sales team? A world-class sales team is one in which the various styles complement each other, each contributing their natural talents to the overall sales effort. And it is more than having the right colour mix – although this is one critical component in a great sales team.

A great sales team – even a good sales team – is one in which everyone works together towards the achievement of a common objective. Sales problems get solved. Customers are served as efficiently as possible by matching their styles and their needs with the most suitable styles and competencies of the sales team members. Meeting and exceeding customer expectations is the driving force of an excellent sales team. To meet and exceed their sales goals, many teams realise that some colours are better as "hunters", doing such tasks as prospecting, developing new business (Red and Yellow), and some are more comfortable as "farmers", doing such tasks as key account management, follow-up and follow-through (Green and Blue). The level of awareness and relationship between the individual members of the team must be very high to achieve this kind of sales team synergy. Each member of the team bears responsibility and makes every effort in the pursuit of common goals. Everyone can sell!

Each of the eight main types has special natural and learned attributes from which the team can profit. However, the pivotal role – the anchor-person – in top-performing sales teams is the sales manager. Their job is to get every style to maximise the full personal and professional potential. But the job of sales manager is more than this. It is also to ensure that appropriate aspects of the selling function are matched to the best styles. Horses for courses! Team selling can be twice as motivating as being an all-round generalist seller. Plus the sales result can be three or four times more productive than the sum of the sales of the individuals working on their own.

WHY DO YOU NEED A GOOD SALES TEAM?

Many sales-driven companies, for example, divide the sales staff into those working inside the company (internal sales) and those working on the road outside the company. Each member of the team is dependent on the others if they want to do their job efficiently. The "travelling" sales representatives maintain direct face-to-face contact with customers, conduct sales meetings and are in direct contact with competitors and the market; the internal sales staff take telephone calls and make sure everything runs smoothly for the customers, such as handling complaints and getting deliveries out on time. Different skills and expertise are required to accomplish these tasks, and it is unlikely that any one person will possess all these skills naturally or be able to employ all these areas of expertise effectively.

Above and beyond the fact that a well-functioning team will carry on the day-to-day business efficiently, it also has the advantage of the various perspectives its individual members can bring that promote improvement. If communication within the team is good and each member of the team has sufficient opportunity to express their opinion, the decisions the team makes will be better. The risk of making mistakes is smaller. Responsibility is shared, and each member of the team can assume the responsibility for the area in which he or she is best qualified.

For the individual members of the team, this increased responsibility means more respect and esteem from the others. A sales representative out on the territory all week can feel that they and the internal staff are connected and part of the same team, and not that one team is "fighting" against the other. The benefits are obvious: Growth and positive development for the individual and the whole business.

What often prevents a team working together effectively is the fact that the individuals who form it have been chosen badly. If a Promoter, for example, is deployed in precise order processing, they will become frustrated after a while, because they are caught up in technical details with too little opportunity to make contacts.

Selecting people who simply do not get on at a personal level is another factor that makes a team less effective. Members of a team often do not get on because each person is capable of seeing only the other's weak points, but not their strengths and talents. They are not aware of the need to appreciate and honour the (colour) difference in other people. Bad communication and a lack of clear sales vision, of course, will just compound the problem.

How do You Put a Good Sales Team Together?

Setting up a sales team is an "empowerment process": The individual members of the team, whether salespeople working outside or inside the office, are given more responsibility and increased powers of decision. This motivates them to work towards the common goals of the team.

If you are the sales manager, you have to be willing to allow the members of your team to participate in its management and thus to focus their natural colour attributes to where they have the best chance to succeed, in this way enabling each member to make their own unique contribution to the team as a whole.

CONDUCTOR	SUPPORTER
competition-oriented	accommodating
likes confrontation	avoids confrontation
direct	constant
result-oriented	shows little emotion
appreciates urgency	adaptable
a doer	good listener
PERSUADER	**CO-ORDINATOR**
process-oriented	product-oriented
open to change	dislikes change
independent	disciplined
optimistic	pessimistic
PROMOTER	**ANALYSER**
trustworthy	exact
not afraid of change	precise
outgoing	quality-conscious
a better speaker than a listener	critical listener
expresses themselves well	communicates non-verbally
self-confident	detail-oriented
RELATOR	**IMPLEMENTOR**
supportive	temperamental
team-oriented	a thinker
constant	creative
co-operative	slow start/fast finish
understanding	

The Eight types and their attributes

WELL-BALANCED TEAMS

Of course, teams whose members are all of the same style have the advantage that their members get to know each other more quickly, get on better and can get projects done faster. They may reach decisions sooner. However, they also tend to make mistakes more easily, as there are a limited number of perspectives available and the decisions made may be one-sided.

Teams with members of different styles, on the other hand, may take longer to reach a decision, but they are better balanced because different perspectives are brought to bear on the situation. These teams make better and more reliable long-term decisions.

Even if a team is confronted with a task that requires that its members should be similar, it is a good idea to add a different style person to the mix. For example, we know a company where a team of five salespeople is responsible for developing a sales territory. The team has two Greens and one each of Blue, Red and Yellow. It works brilliantly because they have found a balance and correct fit for each style. The Red is focused on new calls, prospecting and new business development with bigger clients – his call rate is two per day. The Yellow concentrates on business development with small and medium-sized customers and makes about five calls on average per day. She is excellent at building rapport, getting referrals and getting in the door. The Blue is the Key Account manager, who focuses on the top 20% of customers, because of the ongoing technical requirements of these customers (all the buyers are Blue, by the way). The two Greens do no prospecting at all and focus exclusively on customer retention and maintaining high levels of customer support.

In this team, the individual members have a great chance to grow personally and professionally by learning from the strengths of the other types. Looking at them as they are depicted on the SUCCESS INSIGHTS wheel (**Figure 6**), they move towards the centre: They become more flexible and integrate the strengths and skills of their opposite types in their own behaviour.

The main challenge is to ensure that each member of the team appreciates the work of the others, their way of doing things and their contribution to the overall sales success.

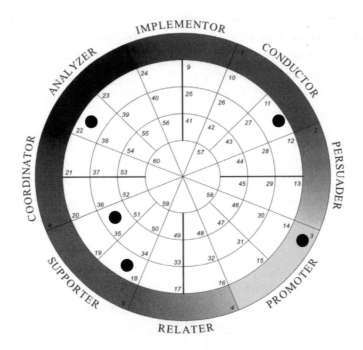

Figure 6: The SUCCESS INSIGHTS wheel with four levels of flexibility and up to 60 positions for exact analysis of character

WHAT CAN THE EIGHT MAIN STYLES CONTRIBUTE TO A TEAM?

A team will make the best decisions if all four styles are involved in the process of decision-making.

Conductor

Contribution: Conductors are single-minded in the pursuit of results and see this as their best contribution to the team. They can ensure that a job is done quickly, either by doing it themselves or by delegating it appropriately. Their talent lies in their ability to spur others on to achieve good results – fellow team-members and customers alike. They work well with systems that ensure sales efficiency – for example, sales automation or organising/diary systems. They make decisions and take control of results. They are discerning, correct, forceful, eloquent, assertive and competition-oriented. For many industries where business development is ongoing and the competition is tough, they are the ideal sales representatives.

Risk: Conductors, however, may exert too much pressure on others and encounter resistance. They do not like discussing their methods and want to do things their own way. They easily become impatient, self-opinionated and suspicious. Once they have set their mind on something, they can be pushy, authoritarian and inconsiderate.

Persuader

Contribution: Persuaders are effective in the field of motivation. Almost at will, they are able to contribute innovative ideas and new strategies on how and where to find new orders and customers. They have a clear picture of the future and a clear plan of how they and the sales team can prepare for it. They see the overall picture. They are pioneering and are always working on new possibilities. This makes Persuaders the ideal strategists in a sales team. They are naturally assertive and their talent for skilful and diplomatic negotiation make them the ideal salesperson to handle difficult customers.

Risk: They may immobilise the team with a constant flood of new ideas. In addition, they may have difficulty in following a concept through to its end and working out all the details. In discussions, they interrupt others whenever they have a new brainwave and are unwilling to go into matters in great detail. They may also lose interest in difficult customers after a while and may not be persistent enough to follow through.

Promoter

Contribution: The Promoter is at home in the fields of interaction and enthusiasm. They can develop ideas and are enthusiastic about the ideas of others. They are good at motivating their team to follow a particular goal, sweeping the others along with their sheer enthusiasm. Their second great attribute is their ability to establish networks. They know lots of people who can be useful to the team. In addition, the Promoter ensures there is fun and entertainment for the team. They are active in organising activities and willing to support other team members openly. They maintain the network of connections between the individual members of the team, bringing people together who otherwise might not get on so easily. They motivate others by means of praise and recognition.

Risk: They are liable to lose sight of the end result. A common criticism of Promoters is that they spend more time "spoofing" than doing. All their energy can easily go into entertaining the team, instead of what they are actually supposed to be doing.

Relator

Contribution: Their forte is dealing with people. Relators sense when individual members of the team are dissatisfied and they naturally respect the needs of others. Their contribution to the overall harmony of the team is immense. They want to ensure that everyone has a fair chance to express their opinion and that no one is passed over. They encourage others to express their opinions openly and genuinely ask them for their opinions. They keep their eye on the human factor at all times. They have no problems accepting other people's decisions or acting on them.

Risk: Sometimes, they become so concerned with the needs of each individual that they forget the task in hand. They assume so much responsibility for others that they begin to finish their sentences for them and get on their nerves with their over-solicitous manner.

Supporter

Contribution: Supporters come into their own in the fields of empathy and sensitivity. They pay attention to the individual members of the team and contribute greatly to a harmonious atmosphere. They give a lot of consideration to what holds the team together, what values it stands for and what convictions it ought to represent. They accept new ideas readily and think about how to put them into action. They will usually have familiarised themselves thoroughly with the field in which they work. They know their market and their customers well. They are ideally suited to looking after customers.

Risk: Supporters can become too set on their own ideas and unable to present any products or schemes that contradict these. They can involve the whole team in endless discussions about underlying ethical questions until they wear everyone out, and if criticised for this, they take offence.

Co-ordinator

Contribution: Co-ordinators are precise and exact. This improves the quality of the work the team does. They are best suited to work behind the scenes, where their organisational talents, cool overview of things, attention to details, understanding of processes and knowledge of the stage of development of every product come into play. They listen easily to others and devote time to them.

Risk: If something goes haywire, they can be very petty. They will harp on the question of who is to blame rather than looking for a solution. Sometimes, they get bogged down in trivialities and lose track of things. They delay responding and deny reality, not realising that denial is one of greatest forms of insult.

Analyser

Contribution: Analysers are precise and detail-oriented. They analyse the concepts of others carefully, and pay attention to details of agreements and offers. They keep their eye on the infrastructure. They conceptualise problems and penetrate quickly to the core of the issues involved.

Risk: Their problem is that they can easily be too theoretical, and then dissatisfied when reality does not match their high expectations. Their reactions are then ineffectual: They get caught up in details and hesitate too long before forming an opinion and expressing it.

Implementor

Contribution: The Implementor's best contribution is that they sometimes give the team the kick it needs to stop it sinking into contemplative harmony and to focus its attention on results. They look at problems logically, weigh up the pros and cons, discover inconsistencies, consider and then act.

Risk: They are sometimes too rough and display their rejection too openly, which does not exactly make them popular with the other members of the team. However, this is not a major concern to them.

CONCLUSION

Individual focused concentration is the very essence of selling! The interpersonal one-on-one relationship between the sales professional and the customer is the live performance in action.

However, there are two aspects of selling that are emerging in professional sales-driven companies that you could adopt. The first is "team selling". This where two, three, even four sales professionals are engaged in a single consultative or strategic sale. How everyone plays their role and style is critical to a successful outcome.

Being part of a sales team as a learning team under the leadership of a sales manager is the second aspect. The team offers huge opportunities for the good to get better and the best to become exceptional. The teacher always learns more than the student – so find every opportunity to help your sales colleagues because it is a win/win.

EPILOGUE

When you do the ordinary things in sales, in an extraordinary way, you will come to *know yourself* and *know your customer* in a very special way. You will reach your goals and be a champion in the ultimate human relations occupation of professional selling.

The first step towards success in any profession is to become totally absorbed in it. ***Know Yourself, Know Your Customer*** gives you an underlying insight into how people "naturally" think, feel and act, and how to connect with more and more people to achieve a win/win result.

Our goal in writing this book is to help you make more sales, faster and easier than ever before. But it is more than that. By becoming a life-long student of human nature, your personal mastery and professional effectiveness, and quality of life will improve dramatically.

A simple, yet powerful exercise, which you can complete right now, is to map your key customers on the SUCCESS INSIGHTS wheel and sell to them as *they* like to buy.

Someone once said: "You can learn a lot by just watching", so become a master listener and keen observer of human behaviour. Write or email us with your real-life stories.

Good luck!

ACKNOWLEDGEMENTS

We would like to express our personal thanks to the following people for their input:

- **Bill Bonnstetter**, without whose 20 years of experience in computerised personality analysis the SUCCESS INSIGHTS wheel would not have been possible.
- **Rick Bowers**, **Dave Bonnstetter** and **Rolando Marchis** at Success Insights International in Arizona have been excellent partners in spreading the Success Insights word around the globe.
- A special thanks to the leaders of Success Insights Europe, who have given us enormous help over the last 10 years. These leaders come from Sweden, Holland, Belgium, Bulgaria, Spain, Portugal, Italy, Great Britain, Ireland, Austria, Germany, Slovenia and Greece.

INDEX

CENTURY MANAGEMENT — DEVELOPING SALES PROFESSIONALS & CULTURES

Your role in selling is one of the most important in the country. Unfortunately, the standard of professionalism in sales is not good. We encourage you, therefore, to embrace the principles of best sales practice and become a sales professional in every respect. *Know Yourself, Know Your Customer* provides you with one fundamental "secret" of sales success – but there are many more.

Please contact us directly at Century Management if you wish to develop superior sales competencies. A career as a top performing sales professional is one of the most challenging, worthwhile and fulfilling jobs in the world.

Century Management helps individuals, teams and organisations to create sales and strategic advantage. Working with a willing and determined individual, it is relatively easy to develop a sales professional. Developing a sales culture where everyone supports the sales effort is more complex but just as achievable.

Around the world, competencies are providing an internal, common framework for organisations to clearly understand what attitudes, values, skills, emotional intelligencies, behaviour benchmarks and learned practices are required to meet their strategic sales objectives. By defining sales competencies, employees, managers and leaders can grasp what is required to reach new levels of excellence and sales performance.

Once the competencies are defined, competency-based tools and applications are designed and implemented. This is the measuring process. They can, in effect, be incorporated into sales training and development initiatives. But not just training – they can also be used for performance appraisals, selection, recruitment and interviewing, promotion planning, career development, and even sales remuneration strategies.

Please write to John Butler or Frank Scheelen at Century Management, Century House, Newlands Business Park, Newlands Cross, Dublin 22, Ireland. Telephone: 00 353 1 4595950, Email: butlerj@century-management.ie.

Other Sales titles from
OAK TREE PRESS

Coaching Champions: How to Bring Out the Absolute Best in Your Salespeople
Frank Salisbury, Cariona Neary & Karl O'Connor
€25 pb : ISBN 1-86076-203-4

Coaching Champions provides all sales managers, from executive level to first-line manager, with tools and techniques to develop their sales people into star performers. Using the POWER coaching method, the authors show that coaching is a much more powerful tool than mere training and that remarkable results will occur.

Win-Win Sales Management: A Powerful New Approach for Increasing Sales from Your Team
Pat Weymes €25 hb : ISBN 1-86076-165-8

While there is a lot of advice available for salespeople, there is little advice for those who train and manage the sales force. In his new book, Pat Weymes outlines a powerful new approach for anyone faced with the task of increasing sales. The win–win approach is based on creating a series of mutually beneficial relationships between all the parties involved, matching the needs of the customer with the company's products or services.

Winning Business Proposals, 3rd edition
Deiric McCann €25 pb : ISBN 1-86076-166-6

This book provides a step-by-step guide through the entire proposal process and includes a unique suite of software, "AutoPropose", to take the work out of producing professional-looking proposals. Aimed at senior managers in any business-to-business environment, **Winning Business Proposals** will provide a competitive advantage that will dramatically increase the quality — and quantity — of your business.

Customer Continuum: Strategic Key Account Management
Deiric McCann €45 pb : ISBN 1-86076-096-1

This Management Briefing introduces the "Customer Continuum", a powerful and original key account development and management mechanism that will help you to decide when an intensive, relationship-based sales approach is appropriate. Accompanied by numerous case studies, these tools will dramatically change the way you manage and value your most important accounts.

To order or for more information, contact:
OAK TREE PRESS
19 Rutland Street, Cork, Ireland
T: + 353 21 431 3855 F: + 353 21 431 3496
E: orders@oaktreepress.com W: www.oaktreepress.com